FEELING
IS THE
SECRET

The Classic Guide to Creating
the Life You Desire

NEVILLE
GODDARD

ST. MARTIN'S
ESSENTIALS
NEW YORK

Published in the United States by St. Martin's Essentials, an imprint of St. Martin's Publishing Group

FOREWORD. Copyright © 2024 by Michelle Wadleigh. All rights reserved. Printed in the United States of America. For information, address St. Martin's Publishing Group, 120 Broadway, New York, NY 10271.

www.stmartins.com

Designed by Steven Seighman

The Library of Congress Cataloging-in-Publication Data is available upon request.

ISBN 978-1-250-34160-0 (trade paperback)
ISBN 978-1-250-34161-7 (ebook)

Our books may be purchased in bulk for promotional, educational, or business use. Please contact your local bookseller or the Macmillan Corporate and Premium Sales Department at 1-800-221-7945, extension 5442, or by email at MacmillanSpecialMarkets@macmillan.com.

Feeling Is the Secret was published in 1951
At Your Command was first published in 1939
Your Faith Is Your Fortune was first published in 1941
Awakened Imagination was first published in 1954

First St. Martin's Essentials Edition: 2024

10 9 8 7 6 5 4 3 2 1

This edition seeks to faithfully reproduce the original publications of the author's works, and so has maintained the original spelling and grammar throughout, with only minor alterations for clarity or content.

CONTENTS

FOREWORD

As a longtime student of the books by Neville Goddard, and a particular fan of his book *Feeling Is the Secret*, I was delighted to be asked to write this foreword. It allowed me the opportunity to immerse myself once more in Neville's teachings—a journey that rekindles a profound sense of awe and resonance within me. What a lovely surprise to find one of his shorter works that I had not yet read, *Your Faith Is Your Future*, was included. To find something I had not yet read by an author I consider a teacher is a true gift. Neville's approach is distinctively natural and intuitive, it aligns with a logic and truth that stirs a deep excitement for the mystical sensibilities that sing to my soul.

Neville Goddard (1905–1972), or just "Neville" as he is most commonly known these days, was born and raised on the Caribbean island of Barbados in the West Indies. He stands apart from others as a colossal figure in the field of metaphysics, albeit one whose acclaim has yet to match his monumental insights. He is an unsung hero. Were he amongst us in this digital age, where social media dominates our homes, I have little doubt that his profound teachings would captivate the global consciousness, and influence the teachings of today's metaphysical teachers, should they know of his work.

You could read his teachings with skepticism, but I have personally seen in my students the impact of his instructions as well as using his work for my own personal experience. Two specific offerings of his work, that is, the use of imagination combined with cultivating feelings, are present in the work of many of today's authors who often do not credit him. My own teaching and writings contain ideas and practices for my students directly based on Neville's influence.

In an age overcrowded with self-proclaimed experts and so-called influencers all too eager to monetize wisdom, Neville navigated in a different era. His was an era which was devoid of the platforms and prestige that so readily amplify voices today. Yet, despite these limitations, his following expanded. One might wonder from whence his influence sprang, what wells of wisdom he drew from, what sparked the light he shared?

Neville was a teacher of metaphysics, and metaphysical teachings can often seem very cerebral and disconnected from the emotional heart-space that is so important in Neville's book, *Feeling Is the Secret*. We need to celebrate the fact that Neville infused these metaphysical teachings with a palpable warmth. He implored us to engage not just in thought, but in the richness of *feeling*—to embrace the emotional resonance of our words and the profound depths of our aspirations.

The metaphysical realm has an emphasis on verbal affirmations and mental discipline, and often it omits the necessary element of emotion. Readers are often told to just "think" something and it'll appear. But when "thinking" alone doesn't magically create their desires, they wonder what was missing, what went wrong? For Neville, *thinking* must be matched with *feeling*. Neville championed the notion that to manifest, one must not only articulate but also resonate deeply with the frequency of feeling. His clarity on this matter was nothing short of revelatory.

Among the numerous gifts you'll find in Neville's powerful teachings included in this volume, one that particularly stands apart is his equating of imagination with the Divine. To Neville, imagination was not merely a faculty of the mind; it was the embodiment of a supreme essence. Using your imagination is a way to access the ideas and inspiration of the Divine in your life. The implication of this idea runs deep in many metaphysical and spiritual schools of thought. Even the book and movie, *The Secret*, which mention Neville as an influence, spoke powerfully about how necessary it is to "feel" into the reality you are seeking to manifest. In celebrating Neville Goddard, we not only honor a man and his philosophy but also reawaken within ourselves to the transformative power of imagination—the divine spark that ignites the potential of our fullest life expression.

Neville's teaching was shaped by a life as colorful and diverse as the teachings he imparted. Born into a large family in 1905 Barbados, Neville's formative years were infused with the rich cultural and spiritual tapestry of the Caribbean, which sowed the early seeds of his expansive worldview. You can imagine the beautiful influence of a culture and group of people who lived so close in harmony with the Earth. In Neville's early adult years, he moved to New York City to pursue his interest in drama and dance, which exposed him to the arts, while nurturing his later emphasis on visualization and the imaginative process.

Neville also had a transformative encounter with Abdullah, an Ethiopian rabbi steeped in mysticism. Abdullah introduced Neville to metaphysical concepts, the mystical depths of the Bible, and the formidable power of imagination—this mentorship would be instrumental in carving out his future path.

Neville's academic endeavors were not confined to conventional academia. For much of his life, he was self-taught, delving deeply into a wide variety of Judeo-Christian texts and the undercurrents of mysticism. His philosophy was not just theoretical but also deeply personal, rooted in his own life's trials and triumphs with the application of imagination. As he ventured into a career of lecturing, his life experiences validated his teaching and he served not only as a teacher and lecturer, but as a model of his concepts. He captivated his audiences across the country with one of his most central tenets: imagination as the conduit to reality. This is where I connect with his work, and this is what I have used for over twenty-five years with my students, and in my personal life.

Through his prolific writing, he shared his transformative insights; I believe he was truly brilliant. His books echoed the essence of his spoken word—intimate, profound, and always aiming to unravel the intricate link between the mind, heart, and emotion. Neville Goddard's legacy, thus, is not just a collection of teachings but an enduring invitation to explore the boundless depth of one's inner landscape.

Just look at the variety of metaphysical thought reflected in the titles of his many books, four of which are included in this compilation (those in bold): *At Your Command* **(1939)**, *Your Faith Is Your Fortune* **(1941)**, Freedom for ALL: A Practical Application of the Bible (1942), *Feeling Is the Secret* **(1944)**,

Prayer: The Art of Believing (1945), *Out of this World: Thinking Fourth-Dimensionally* (1949), *The Power of Awareness* (1952), **Awakened Imagination/The Search** (1954), *Seedtime and Harvest: A Mystical View of the Scriptures* (1956), *The Law and the Promise* (1961), and *Resurrection* (1966).

If you follow Neville's lead in cultivating an understanding of emotions as it applies to your desired outcomes, you will find yourself steeped in a practical spirituality that stands out from the rest. I want to share with you a short story that demonstrates his work in use.

Samantha was a fledgling writer with dreams bigger than her reality. Encountering Neville Goddard's teachings was like finding a road map to the treasures of her own mind. Neville spoke of the power of imagination, of living in the end, and of feeling of the wish fulfilled.

Taking this to heart, Samantha began a simple nightly routine. Each night before sleep, she would visualize herself as a successful writer. She felt the weight of her published book in her hands, heard the praise from her readers, and saw her name on the bestseller list.

Months went by. The exercise seemed only that—just an exercise. But as she persisted, imagining her inner world rich with the success she yearned for, her emotions (feelings) were cultivated. Then, almost magically, the outer world began to align with her inner. An editor expressed interest in her blog, a literary agent reached out to her, and before she knew it, Samantha was holding the first copy of her own novel, just as she had imagined.

The change was so gradual yet so sure, it felt like a dream made real. Samantha knew it was the fruit of her disciplined imagination, a testament to Neville's teachings. She had lived in the end, in the end had become her beginning.

Could Samantha have accomplished her dream without the practice of imaging? Possibly. But there is a bonus that comes from using Neville's teaching that is a bit less obvious, and that is when you invest your time and energy imagining your desired outcome, it also impacts your sense of well-being and self-confidence because it causes you to believe in yourself.

Science and metaphysics are in closer relationship than at any time in history. Science seems to be proving the principles and power of the mind *and* the imagination more every year. For this reason, reading this compilation of Neville's works will support you in feeling ready to dream your dream and expect potent and demonstrable results. I hope you feel as empowered and enthusiastic about Neville's work as I have. If you are a spiritual teacher, therapist, or coach, you will find his work to be a powerful support in the work that you do. And for all readers who are open to these life-changing ideas, this collection of titles by this "teacher of teachers" will inspire you to *feel* your passions and dreams. Immerse yourself in these rich and wise ideas, try them out for yourself, and see how you can *imagine* your own best life.

—Rev. Dr. Michelle Wadleigh

FEELING
IS THE
SECRET

FEELING IS THE SECRET

by

Neville

1951

Of making many books there is no end.

—Ecclesiastes 12:12

He that would perfect himself in any art whatsoever, let him betake himself to the reading of some sure and certain work upon his art many times over; for to read many books upon your art produceth confusion rather than learning.

—Old saying

CONTENTS

FOREWORD

This book is concerned with the art of realizing your desire. It gives you an account of the mechanism used in the production of the visible world. It is a small book but not slight. There is a treasure in it, a clearly defined road to the realization of your dreams.

Were it possible to carry conviction to another by means of reasoned arguments and detailed instances, this book would be many times its size. It is seldom possible, however, to do so by means of written statements or arguments since to the suspended judgment it always seems plausible to say that the author was dishonest or deluded, and, therefore, his evidence was tainted. Consequently, I have purposely omitted all arguments and testimonials, and simply challenge the open-minded reader to practice the law of consciousness as revealed in this book.

Personal success will prove far more convincing than all the books that could be written on the subject.

—Neville

1

LAW AND ITS OPERATION

The world, and all within it, is man's conditioned consciousness objectified. Consciousness is the cause as well as the substance of the entire world.

So it is to consciousness that we must turn if we would discover the secret of creation.

Knowledge of the law of consciousness and the method of operating this law will enable you to accomplish all you desire in life.

Armed with a working knowledge of this law, you can build and maintain an ideal world.

Consciousness is the one and only reality, not figuratively but actually. This reality may for the sake of clarity be likened unto a stream which is divided into two parts, the conscious and the subconscious.

In order to intelligently operate the law of consciousness, it is necessary to understand the relationship between the conscious and the subconscious.

The conscious is personal and selective; the subconscious is impersonal and non-selective. The conscious is the realm of effect; the subconscious is the realm of cause. These two aspects are the male and female divisions of consciousness. The conscious is male; the subconscious is female.

The conscious generates ideas and impresses these ideas on the subconscious; the subconscious receives ideas and gives form and expression to them.

By this law—first conceiving an idea and then impressing the idea conceived on the subconscious—all things evolve out of consciousness; and without this sequence, there is not anything made that is made.

The conscious impresses the subconscious, while the subconscious expresses all that is impressed upon it.

The subconscious does not originate ideas, but accepts as true those which the conscious mind feels to be true and, in a way known only to itself, objectifies the accepted ideas.

Therefore, through his power to imagine and feel and his freedom to choose the idea he will entertain, man has control over creation. Control of the subconscious is accomplished through control of your ideas and feelings.

The mechanism of creation is hidden in the very depth of the subconscious, the female aspect or womb of creation.

The subconscious transcends reason and is independent of induction. It contemplates a feeling as a fact existing within itself and on this assumption proceeds to give expression to it. The creative process begins with an idea and its cycle runs its course as a feeling and ends in a volition to act.

Ideas are impressed on the subconscious through the medium of feeling.

No idea can be impressed on the subconscious until it is felt, but once felt—be it good, bad or indifferent—it must be expressed.

Feeling is the one and only medium through which ideas are conveyed to the subconscious.

Therefore, the man who does not control his feeling may easily impress the subconscious with undesirable states. By control of feeling is not meant restraint or suppression of your feeling, but rather the disciplining of self to imagine and entertain only such feeling as contributes to your happiness.

Control of your feeling is all important to a full and happy life.

Never entertain an undesirable feeling, nor think sympathetically about wrong in any shape or form. Do not dwell on the imperfection of yourself or others. To do so is to impress the subconscious with these limitations. What you do not want done unto you, do not feel that it is done unto you or another. This is the whole law of a full and happy life. Everything else is commentary.

Every feeling makes a subconscious impression and, unless it is counteracted by a more powerful feeling of an opposite nature, must be expressed.

The dominant of two feelings is the one expressed. *I am healthy* is a stronger feeling than *I will be healthy*. To feel *I will be* is to confess *I am not*; *I am* is stronger than *I am not*.

What you feel *you are* always dominates what you feel *you would like to be*; therefore, to be realized, the wish must be felt as *a state that is* rather than *a state that is not*.

Sensation precedes manifestation and is the foundation upon which all manifestation rests. Be careful of your moods and feelings, for there is an unbroken connection between your feelings and your visible world. Your body is an emotional filter and bears the unmistakable marks of your prevalent emotions. Emotional disturbances, especially suppressed emotions, are the causes of all disease. To feel intensely about a wrong without voicing or expressing that feeling is the beginning of disease—dis-ease—in both body and environment. Do not entertain the feeling of regret or failure for frustration or detachment from your objective results in disease.

Think feelingly only of the state you desire to realize. Feeling the reality of the state sought and living and acting on that conviction is the way of all seeming miracles. All changes of expression are brought about through a change of feeling. A change of feeling is a change of destiny. All creation occurs in the domain of the subconscious. What you must acquire, then, is a reflective control of the operation of the subconscious, that is, control of your ideas and feelings.

Chance or accident is not responsible for the things that happen to you, nor is predestined fate the author of your fortune or misfortune. Your subconscious impressions determine the conditions of your world. The subconscious is not selective; it is impersonal and no respecter of persons [Acts 10:34; Rom. 2:11]. The subconscious is not concerned with the truth or falsity of your feeling. It always accepts as true that which you feel to be true. Feeling is the assent of the subconscious to the truth of that which is declared to be true. Because of this quality of the subconscious there is nothing impossible to man. Whatever the mind of man can conceive and feel as true, the subconscious can and must objectify. Your feelings create the pattern from which your world is fashioned, and a change of feeling is a change of pattern.

The subconscious never fails to express that which has been impressed upon it.

The moment it receives an impression, it begins to work out the ways of its expression. It accepts the feeling impressed upon it, your feeling, as a fact existing within itself and immediately sets about to produce in the outer or objective world the exact likeness of that feeling.

The subconscious never alters the accepted beliefs of man. It out-pictures them to the last detail whether or not they are beneficial.

To impress the subconscious with the desirable state, you must assume the feeling that would be yours had you already realized your wish. In defining your objective, you must be concerned only with the objective itself. The manner of expression or the difficulties involved are not to be considered by you. To think feelingly on any state impresses it on the subconscious. Therefore, if you dwell on difficulties, barriers or delay, the subconscious, by its very nonselective nature, accepts the feeling of difficulties and obstacles as your request and proceeds to produce them in your outer world.

The subconscious is the womb of creation. It receives the idea unto itself through the feelings of man. It never changes the idea received, but always gives it form. Hence the subconscious out-pictures the idea in the image and likeness of the feeling received. To feel a state as hopeless or impossible is to impress the subconscious with the idea of failure.

Although the subconscious faithfully serves man, it must not be inferred that the relation is that of a servant to a master as was anciently conceived. The ancient prophets called it the slave and servant of man. St. Paul personified it as a "woman" and said: "The woman should be subject to man in everything" [Eph. 5:24; also, 1 Cor. 14:34, Eph. 5:22, Col. 3:18, 1 Peter 3:1]. The subconscious does serve man and faithfully gives form to his feelings. However, the subconscious has a distinct distaste for compulsion and responds to persuasion rather than to command; consequently, it resembles the beloved wife more than the servant.

"The husband is head of the wife," Ephesians 5:23, may not be true of man and woman in their earthly relationship, but it is true of the conscious and the subconscious, or the male and female aspects of consciousness. The mystery to which Paul referred when he wrote, "This is a great mystery [5:32] . . . He that loveth his wife loveth himself [5:28] . . . And they two shall be one flesh [5:31]", is simply the mystery of consciousness. Consciousness is really one and undivided but for creation's sake it appears to be divided into two.

The conscious (objective) or male aspect truly is the head and dominates the subconscious (subjective) or female aspect.

However, this leadership is not that of the tyrant, but of the lover.

So, by assuming the feeling that would be yours were you already in possession of your objective, the subconscious is moved to build the exact likeness of your assumption.

Your desires are not subconsciously accepted until you assume the feeling of their reality, for only through feeling is an idea subconsciously accepted and only through this subconscious acceptance is it ever expressed.

It is easier to ascribe your feeling to events in the world than to admit that the conditions of the world reflect your feeling. However, it is eternally true that the outside mirrors the inside.

"As within, so without" *["As above, so below; as below, so above; as within, so without, as without, so within"* ("Correspondence", the second of The Seven Principles of Hermes Trismegistus)*]*.

"A man can receive nothing unless it is given him from heaven" [John 3:27] and "The kingdom of heaven is within you" [Luke 17:21]. Nothing comes from without; all things come from within—from the subconscious.

It is impossible for you to see other than the contents of your consciousness. Your world in its every detail is your consciousness objectified. Objective states bear witness of subconscious impressions. A change of impression results in a change of expression.

The subconscious accepts as true that which you feel as true, and because creation is the result of subconscious impressions, you, by your feeling, determine creation.

You are already that which you want to be, and your refusal to believe this is the only reason you do not see it.

To seek on the outside for that which you do not feel you are is to seek in vain, for we never find that which we want; we find only that which we are.

In short, you express and have only that which you are conscious of being or possessing. "To him that hath it is given" [Matt. 13:12, 25:29; Mark 4:25; Luke 8:18, 19:26]. Denying the evidence of the senses and appropriating the feeling of the wish fulfilled is the way to the realization of your desire.

Mastery of self-control of your thoughts and feelings is your highest achievement.

However, until perfect self-control is attained, so that, in spite of appearances, you feel all that you want to feel, use sleep and prayer to aid you in realizing your desired states.

These are the two gateways into the subconscious.

2

SLEEP

S leep, the life that occupies one-third of our stay on earth, is the natural door into the subconscious.

So it is with sleep that we are now concerned. The conscious two-thirds of our life on earth is measured by the degree of attention we give sleep. Our understanding of and delight in what sleep has to bestow will cause us, night after night, to set out for it as though we were keeping an appointment with a lover.

"In a dream, in a vision of the night, when deep sleep falleth upon men, in slumbering upon the bed; then he openeth the ears of men and sealeth their instruction" [Job 33].

It is in sleep and in prayer, a state akin to sleep, that man enters the subconscious to make his impressions and receive his instructions. In these states the conscious and subconscious are creatively joined. The male and female become one flesh. Sleep is the time when the male or conscious mind turns from the world of sense to seek its lover or subconscious self.

The subconscious—unlike the woman of the world who marries her husband to change him—has no desire to change the conscious, waking state, but loves it as it is and faithfully reproduces its likeness in the outer world of form.

The conditions and events of your life are your children formed from the molds of your subconscious impressions in sleep. They are made in the image and likeness of your innermost feeling that they may reveal you to yourself.

"As in heaven, so on earth" [Matt. 6:10; Luke 11:2]. As in the subconscious, so on earth.

Whatever you have in consciousness as you go to sleep is the measure of your expression in the waking two-thirds of your life on earth.

Nothing stops you from realizing your objective save your failure to feel that you are already that which you wish to be, or that you are already in possession of the thing sought. Your subconscious gives form to your desires only when you feel your wish fulfilled.

The unconsciousness of sleep is the normal state of the subconscious. Because all things come from within yourself, and your conception of yourself determines that which comes, you should always feel the wish fulfilled before you drop off to sleep.

You never draw out of the deep of yourself that which you want; you always draw that which you are, and you are that which you feel yourself to be as well as that which you feel as true of others.

To be realized, then, the wish must be resolved into the feeling of being or having or witnessing the state sought. This is accomplished by assuming the feeling of the wish fulfilled. The feeling which comes in response to the question "How would I feel were my wish realized?" is the feeling which should monopolize and immobilize your attention as you relax into sleep. You must be in the consciousness of being or having that which you want to be or to have before you drop off to sleep.

Once asleep, man has no freedom of choice. His entire slumber is dominated by his last waking concept of self.

It follows, therefore, that he should always assume the feeling of accomplishment and satisfaction before he retires in sleep, "Come before me with singing and thanksgiving" [Ps. 95:2], "Enter into his gates with thanksgiving and into his courts with praise" [Ps. 100:4]. Your mood prior to sleep defines your state of consciousness as you enter into the presence of your everlasting lover, the subconscious.

She sees you exactly as you feel yourself to be. If, as you prepare for sleep, you assume and maintain the consciousness of success by feeling "I am successful", you must be successful. Lie flat on your back with your head on a level with your body. Feel as you would were you in possession of your wish and quietly relax into unconsciousness.

"He that keepeth Israel shall neither slumber nor sleep" [Ps. 121:4]. Nevertheless "He giveth his beloved sleep" [Ps. 127:2].

The subconscious never sleeps. Sleep is the door through which the conscious, waking mind passes to be creatively joined to the subconscious.

Sleep conceals the creative act, while the objective world reveals it.

In sleep, man impresses the subconscious with his conception of himself.

What more beautiful description of this romance of the conscious and subconscious is there than that told in the "Song of Solomon": "By night on my bed I sought him whom my soul loveth [3:1] . . . I found him whom my soul loveth; I held him and I not let him go, until I had brought him into my mother's house, and into the chamber of her that conceived me" [3:4].

Preparing to sleep, you feel yourself into the state of the answered wish, and then relax into unconsciousness. Your realized wish is he whom you seek. By night, on your bed, you seek the feeling of the wish fulfilled that you may take it with you into the chamber of her that conceived you, into sleep or the subconscious which gave you form, that this wish also may be given expression.

This is the way to discover and conduct your wishes into the subconscious. Feel yourself in the state of the realized wish and quietly drop off to sleep.

Night after night, you should assume the feeling of being, having and witnessing that which you seek to be, possess and see manifested. Never go to sleep feeling discouraged or dissatisfied. Never sleep in the consciousness of failure.

Your subconscious, whose natural state is sleep, sees you as you believe yourself to be, and whether it be good, bad or indifferent, the subconscious will faithfully embody your belief.

As you feel so do you impress her; and she, the perfect lover, gives form to these impressions and out-pictures them as the children of her beloved.

"Thou art all fair, my love; there is no spot in thee" [Song of Sol. 4:7] is the attitude of mind to adopt before dropping off to sleep.

Disregard appearances and feel that things are as you wish them to be, for "He calleth things that are not seen as though they were, and the unseen becomes seen" [approx.; Rom. 4:17]. To assume the feeling of satisfaction is to call conditions into being which will mirror satisfaction.

"Signs follow, they do not precede".

Proof that you are will follow the consciousness that you are; it will not precede it.

You are an eternal dreamer dreaming non-eternal dreams. Your dreams take form as you assume the feeling of their reality.

Do not limit yourself to the past.

Knowing that nothing is impossible to consciousness, begin to imagine states beyond the experiences of the past.

Whatever the mind of man can imagine, man can realize. All objective (visible) states were first subjective (invisible) states, and you called them into visible by assuming the feeling of their reality.

The creative process is first imagining and then believing the state imagined. Always imagine and expect the best.

The world cannot change until you change your conception of it. "As within, so without".

Nations, as well as people, are only what you believe them to be. No matter what the problem is, no matter where it is, no matter whom it concerns, you have no one to change but yourself, and you have neither opponent nor helper in bringing about the change within yourself. You have nothing to do but convince yourself of the truth of that which you desire to see manifested.

As soon as you succeed in convincing yourself of the reality of the state sought, results follow to confirm your fixed belief. You never suggest to another the state which you desire to see him express; instead, you convince yourself that he is already that which you desire him to be.

Realization of your wish is accomplished by assuming the feeling of the wish fulfilled. You cannot fail unless you fail to convince yourself of the reality of your wish. A change of belief is confirmed by a change of expression.

Every night, as you drop off to sleep, feel satisfied and spotless, for your subjective lover always forms the objective world in the image and likeness of your conception of it, the conception defined by your feeling.

The waking two-thirds of your life on earth ever corroborates or bears witness to your subconscious impressions. The actions and events of the day are effects; they are not causes. Free will is only freedom of choice.

"Choose ye this day whom ye shall serve" [Josh. 24:15] is your freedom to choose the kind of mood you assume; but the expression of the mood is the secret of the subconscious.

The subconscious receives impressions only through the feelings of man and, in a way known only to itself, gives these impressions form and expression. The actions of man are determined by his subconscious impressions.

His illusion of free will, his belief in freedom of action, is but ignorance of the causes which make him act. He thinks himself free because he has forgotten the link between himself and the event.

Man awake is under compulsion to express his subconscious impressions. If in the past he unwisely impressed himself, then let him begin to change his thought and feeling, for only as he does so will he change his world. Do not waste one moment in regret, for to think feelingly of the mistakes of the past is to reinfect yourself. "Let the dead bury the dead" [Matt. 8:22; Luke 9:60]. Turn from appearances and assume the feeling that would be yours were you already the one you wish to be.

Feeling a state produces that state.

The part you play on the world's stage is determined by your conception of yourself.

By feeling your wish fulfilled and quietly relaxing into sleep, you cast yourself in a star role to be played on earth tomorrow, and, while asleep, you are rehearsed and instructed in your part.

The acceptance of the end automatically wills the means of realization. Make no mistake about this. If, as you prepare for sleep, you do not consciously feel yourself into the state of the answered wish, then you will take with you into the chamber of her who conceived you the sum total of the reactions and feelings of the waking day; and while asleep, you will be instructed in the manner in which they will be expressed tomorrow. You will rise believing that you are a free agent, not realizing that every action and event of the day is predetermined by your concept of self as you fell asleep. Your only freedom, then, is your freedom of reaction. You are free to choose how you feel and react to the day's drama, but the drama—the actions, events and circumstances of the day—have already been determined.

Unless you consciously and purposely define the attitude of mind with which you go to sleep, you unconsciously go to sleep in the composite attitude of mind made up of all feelings and reactions of the day. Every reaction makes a subconscious impression and, unless counteracted by an opposite and more dominant feeling, is the cause of future action.

Ideas enveloped in feeling are creative actions. Use your divine right wisely. Through your ability to think and feel, you have dominion over all creation.

While you are awake, you are a gardener selecting seed for your garden, but "Except a corn of wheat fall into the ground and die, it abideth alone; but if it die, it bringeth forth much fruit" [John 12:24]. Your conception of yourself as you fall asleep is the seed you drop into the ground of the subconscious. Dropping off to sleep feeling satisfied and happy compels conditions and events to appear in your world which confirm these attitudes of mind.

Sleep is the door into heaven. What you take in as a feeling you bring out as a condition, action, or object in space. So sleep in the feeling of the wish fulfilled.

"As in consciousness, so on earth."

] **3** [

PRAYER

Prayer, like sleep, is also an entrance into the subconscious. "When you pray, enter into your closet, and when you have shut your door, pray to your Father which is in secret and your Father which is in secret shall reward you openly" [Matt. 6:6].

Prayer is an illusion of sleep which diminishes the impression of the outer world and renders the mind more receptive to suggestion from within. The mind in prayer is in a state of relaxation and receptivity akin to the feeling attained just before dropping off to sleep.

Prayer is not so much what you ask for, as how you prepare for its reception. "Whatsoever things ye desire, when ye pray believe that you have received them, and ye shall have them" [Mark 11:24].

The only condition required is that you believe that your prayers are already realized.

Your prayer must be answered if you assume the feeling that would be yours were you already in possession of your objective. The moment you accept the wish as an accomplished fact, the subconscious finds means for its realization. To pray successfully then, you must yield to the wish, that is, feel the wish fulfilled.

The perfectly disciplined man is always in tune with the wish as an accomplished fact.

He knows that consciousness is the one and only reality, that ideas and feelings are facts of consciousness and are as real as objects in space; therefore he never entertains a feeling which does not contribute to his happiness, for feelings are the causes of the actions and circumstances of his life.

On the other hand, the undisciplined man finds it difficult to believe that which is denied by the senses and usually accepts or rejects solely on appearances of the senses. Because of this tendency to rely on the evidence of the senses, it is necessary to shut them out before starting to pray, before attempting to feel that which they deny. Whenever you are in the state of mind "I should like to, but I cannot", the harder you try, the less you are able to yield to the wish. You never attract that which you want, but always attract that which you are conscious of being.

Prayer is the art of assuming the feeling of being and having that which you want.

When the senses confirm the absence of your wish, all conscious effort to counteract this suggestion is futile and tends to intensify the suggestion.

Prayer is the art of yielding to the wish and not the forcing of the wish. Whenever your feeling is in conflict with your wish, feeling will be the victor. The dominant feeling invariably expresses itself. Prayer must be without effort. In attempting to fix an attitude of mind which is denied by the senses, effort is fatal.

To yield successfully to the wish as an accomplished fact, you must create a passive state, a kind of reverie or meditative reflection similar to the feeling which precedes sleep. In such a relaxed state, the mind is turned from the objective world and easily senses the reality of a subjective state. It is a state in which you are conscious and quite able to move or open your eyes but have no desire to do so. An easy way to create this passive state is to relax in a comfortable chair or on a bed. If on a bed, lie flat on your back with your head on a level with your body, close the eyes and imagine that you are sleepy. Feel—I am sleepy, so sleepy, so very sleepy.

In a little while, a faraway feeling accompanied by a general lassitude and loss of all desire to move envelops you. You feel a pleasant, comfortable rest and not inclined to alter your position, although under other circumstances you would not be at all comfortable. When this passive state is reached, imagine that you have realized your wish—not how it was realized, but simply the wish fulfilled. Imagine in picture form what you desire to achieve in life; then feel yourself as having already achieved it. Thoughts produce tiny little speech movements which may be heard in the passive state of prayer as pronouncements from without. However, this degree of passivity is not essential to the realization of your prayers. All that is necessary is to create a passive state and feel the wish fulfilled.

All you can possibly need or desire is already yours. You need no helper to give it to you; it is yours now. Call your desires into being by imagining and feeling your wish fulfilled. As the end is accepted, you become totally indifferent as to possible failure, for acceptance of the end wills the means to that end. When you emerge from the moment of prayer, it is as though you were shown the happy and successful end of a play although you were not shown how that end was achieved. However, having witnessed the end, regardless of any anticlimactic sequence, you remain calm and secure in the knowledge that the end has been perfectly defined.

] 4 [

SPIRIT—FEELING

"Not by might, nor by power, but by my spirit, saith the Lord of hosts" [Zech. 4:6]. Get into the spirit of the state desired by assuming the feeling that would be yours were you already the one you want to be. As you capture the feeling of the state sought, you are relieved of all effort to make it so, for it is already so. There is a definite feeling associated with every idea in the mind of man. Capture the feeling associated with your realized wish by assuming the feeling that would be yours were you already in possession of the thing you desire, and your wish will objectify itself.

Faith is feeling, "According to your faith (feeling) be it unto you" [Matt. 9:29]. You never attract that which you want, but always that which you are. As a man is, so does he see. "To him that hath it shall be given and to him that hath not it shall be taken away . . ." [Matt. 13:12, 25:29; Mark 4:25; Luke 8:18, 19:26]. That which you feel yourself to be, you are, and you are given that which you are. So assume the feeling that would be yours were you already in possession of your wish, and your wish must be realized.

"So God created man in his own image, in the image of God created he him" [Gen. 1:27]. "Let this mind be in you which was also in Christ Jesus, who being in the form of God, thought it not robbery to be equal with God" [Phil. 2:5, 6]. You are that which you believe yourself to be.

Instead of believing in God or in Jesus—believe you are God or you are Jesus. "He that believeth on Me, the works that I do shall he do also" [John 14:12] should be "He that believes as I believe the works that I do shall he do also". Jesus found it not strange to do the works of God, because He believed Himself to be God. "I and My Father are one" [John 10:30]. It is natural to do the works of the one you believe yourself to be. So live in the feeling of being the one you want to be and that you shall be.

When a man believes in the value of the advice given him and applies it, he establishes within himself the reality of success.

AT YOUR COMMAND

AT YOUR COMMAND

by

Neville

1939

This book contains the very essence of the Principle of Expression.

Had I cared to, I could have expanded it into a book of several hundred pages, but such expansion would have defeated the purpose of this book.

Commands to be effective—must be short and to the point: the greatest command ever recorded is found in the few simple words, "And God said, "*Let there be light.*"

In keeping with this principle, I now give to you, the reader, in these few pages, the truth, as it was revealed to me.

—*Neville*

AT YOUR COMMAND

Can man decree a thing and have it come to pass? Most decidedly he can! Man has always decreed that which has appeared in his world and is today decreeing that which is appearing in his world and shall continue to do so as long as man is conscious of being man.

Not one thing has ever appeared in man's world but what man decreed that it should.

This you may deny, but try as you will, you cannot disprove it, for this decreeing is based upon a changeless principle.

You do not command things to appear by your words or loud affirmations. Such vain repetition is more often than not confirmation of the opposite.

Decreeing is ever done in consciousness.

That is, every man is conscious of being that which he has decreed himself to be. The dumb man, without using words, is conscious of being dumb. Therefore, he is decreeing himself to be dumb.

When the Bible is read in this light, you will find it to be the greatest scientific book ever written.

Instead of looking upon the Bible as the historical record of an ancient civilization or the biography of the unusual life of Jesus, see it as a great psychological drama taking place in the consciousness of man.

Claim it as your own and you will suddenly transform your world from the barren deserts of Egypt to the promised land of Canaan.

Everyone will agree with the statement that *all things were made by God, and without Him there is nothing made—that is made* [John 1:3]—but, what man does not agree upon is the identity of God.

All the churches and priesthoods of the world disagree as to the identity and true nature of God.

The Bible proves beyond the shadow of a doubt that Moses and the prophets were in one hundred per cent accord as to the identity and nature of God.

And Jesus life and teachings are in agreement with the findings of the prophets of old.

Moses discovered God to be man's *awareness of being,* when he declared these little understood words. *"I AM hath sent me unto you"* [Exod. 3:14].

David sang in his psalms, *"Be still and know that I AM God; I will be exalted in the earth"* [Ps. 46:10]. Isaiah declared, *"I AM the Lord and there is none else. There is no God beside Me. I girded thee, though thou hast not known Me. I form the light, and create darkness; I make peace, and create evil. I, the Lord, do all these things"* [Isa. 45:5–7].

The *awareness of being* as God is stated hundreds of times in the New Testament.

To name but a few: *"I AM the shepherd, I AM the door* [John 10:2, 10:7, 10:9]; *I AM the resurrection and the life* [John 11:25];

I AM the way [John 14:6]; *I AM the Alpha and Omega* [Rev. 1:8, 22:13]; *I AM the beginning and the end*"; and again, "*Whom do you say that I AM?*" [Matt. 16:15; Mark 8:29; Luke 9:20].

It is not stated, "I, Jesus, am the door. I, Jesus, am the way", nor is it said, "Whom do you say that I, Jesus, am?"

It is clearly stated. "*I AM* the way".

The *awareness of being* is the door through which the manifestations of life pass into the world of form.

Consciousness is the resurrecting power—resurrecting that which man is conscious of being.

Man is ever out-picturing that which he is conscious of being.

This is the truth that makes man free [John 8:32], for man is always self-imprisoned or self-freed.

If you, the reader, will give up all of your former beliefs in a God apart from yourself, and claim God as your *awareness of being*—as Jesus and the prophets did—, you will transform your world with the realization that, "*I and My Father are One*" [John 10:30].

This statement, "*I and My Father are one* [John 10:30], *but My Father is greater than I*" [John 14:28] seems very confusing—but if interpreted in the light of what we have just said concerning the identity of God, you will find it very revealing.

Consciousness, being God, is as "Father". The thing that you are conscious of being is the "Son bearing witness of His "Father".

It is like the conceiver and its conceptions. The conceiver is ever greater than his conceptions, yet ever remains one with his conception.

For instance, before you are conscious of being man, you are first conscious of *being*. Then you become conscious of being man. Yet you remain as conceiver, greater than your conception—man.

Jesus discovered this glorious truth and declared Himself to be one with God—not a God that man had fashioned.

For He never recognized such a God.

He said, *"If any man should ever come, saying, "Look here or look there', believe them not, for the kingdom of God is within you"* [*"Neither shall they say, Lo here! or, lo there! for, behold, the kingdom of God is within you"* (Luke 17:21); *"And they shall say to you, See here; or, see there: go not after them, nor follow them"* (Luke 17:23)].

Heaven is within you. Therefore, when it is recorded that *"He went unto His Father"* [*"He was received up into heaven"* (Mark 16:19; Luke 24:51)], it is telling you that He rose in consciousness to the point where He was just conscious of *being*, thus transcending the limitations of His present conception of Himself, called "Jesus".

In the *awareness of being* all things are possible.

He said, *"You shall decree a thing and it shall come to pass"* [Job 22:28].

This is His decreeing—rising in consciousness to the naturalness of being the thing desired.

As He expressed it. *"And I, if I be lifted up. I shall draw all men unto Me"* [*"And I, if I be lifted up from the earth, will draw all men unto Me"* (John 12:32)].

If I be lifted up in consciousness to the naturalness of the thing desired. I will draw the manifestation of that desire unto Me.

For He states. *"No man comes unto Me save the Father within*

Me draws him" [John 6:44], *and "I and My Father are one"* [John 10:30].

Therefore, consciousness is the Father that is drawing the manifestations of life unto you.

You are, at this very moment, drawing into your world that which you are now conscious of being.

Now you can see what is meant by, "You must be born again" [John 3:7].

If you are dissatisfied with your present expression in life, the only way to change it is to take your attention away from that which seems so real to you and rise in consciousness to that which you desire to be.

You cannot serve two masters [Matt. 6:24; Luke 16:13], therefore, to take your attention from one state of consciousness and place it upon another is to die to one and live to the other.

The question *"Whom do you say that I am?"* [Matt. 16:13; Mark 8:29; Luke 9:20] is not addressed to a man called "Peter" by one called "Jesus".

This is the eternal question addressed to ones self by one's true being.

In other words, "Whom do you say that you are?".

For your conviction of yourself—your opinion of yourself—will determine your expression in life.

He states, *"You believe in God—believe also in Me"* [John 14:1].

In other words, it is the *Me* within you that is this God.

***Praying, then, is seen to be recognizing yourself to *be* that which you now desire, rather than its accepting form of petitioning a God that does not exist for that which you now desire.

So can't you see why the millions of prayers are unanswered? Men pray to a God that does not exist.

For instance: To be conscious of being poor and to pray to a God for riches is to be rewarded with that which you are conscious of being—which is poverty.

Prayers, to be successful, *must be claiming* rather than begging—so if you would pray for riches, turn from your picture of poverty by denying the very evidence of your senses and assume the nature of being wealthy.

We are told, "When you pray, go within in secret and shut the door. And that which your Father sees in secret, with that will He reward you openly" [Matt. 6:6].

We have identified the "Father to be the *awareness of being*".

We have also identified the "door to be the *awareness of being*".

> So "shutting the door" is shutting out that which "I" am
> now aware of being and claiming myself to be that which
> "I" desire to be.

The very moment my claim is established to the point of conviction, that moment I begin to draw unto myself the evidence of my claim.

Do not question the how of these things appearing, for no man knows that way. That is, no manifestation knows how the things desired will appear.

Consciousness is the way or door through which things appear.

He said, *"I AM the way"* [John 14:6]—not "I, John Smith, am the way, but *"I AM"*, the *awareness of being*, is the way through which the thing shall come. The signs always follow. They never precede.

Things have no reality other than in consciousness.

Therefore, get the consciousness first and the thing is compelled to appear.

You are told, *"Seek ye first the kingdom of Heaven and all things shall be added unto you"* [Matt. 6:33].

Get first the consciousness of the things that you are seeking and leave the things alone. This is what is meant by "Ye shall decree a thing and it shall come to pass" [Job 22:28].

Apply this principle and you will know what it is to *"prove Me and see"* [*"prove Me now herewith, saith the LORD of hosts, if I will not open you the windows of heaven, and pour you out a blessing, that there shall not be room enough to receive it"* (Mal. 3:10)].

The story of Mary is the story of every man.

Mary was not a woman—giving birth in some miraculous way to one called "Jesus".

Mary is the *awareness of being* that ever remains virgin, no matter how many desires it gives birth to.

Right now, look upon yourself as this Virgin Mary—being impregnated by yourself through the medium of desire—becoming one with your desire to the point of embodying or giving birth to your desire.

For instance: it is said of Mary (whom you now know to be yourself) that *she know not a man* [Luke 1:34]. *Yet she conceived.*

That is, you. John Smith, have no reason to believe that that which you now desire is possible, but having discovered your *awareness of being* to be God, you make this awareness your husband and conceive a man child (manifestation) of the Lord,

"For thy maker is thine husband; the Lord of hosts is His Name; the Lord God of the whole earth shall He be called" [Isa. 54:5].

Your ideal or ambition is this conception—the first command to her, which is now to yourself, is *"Go, tell no man"* [before: Mark 1:44; after: Matt. 8:4, Luke 5:14].

That is, do not discuss your ambitions or desires with another, for the other will only echo your present fears.

Secrecy is the first law to be observed in realizing your desire.

The second, as we are told in the story of Mary, is to *"Magnify the Lord"* [Luke 1:46].

We have identified the *Lord* as your *awareness of being*.

Therefore, to "magnify the Lord" is to revalue or expand one's present conception of one's self to the point where this revaluation becomes natural.

When this naturalness is attained, you give birth by becoming that which you are one with in consciousness.

The story of creation is given us in digest form in the first chapter of John.

"In the beginning was the word" [John 1:1]. Now, this very second, is the "beginning" spoken of. It is the beginning of an urge—a desire.

"The word" is the desire swimming around in your consciousness—seeking embodiment.

The urge of itself has no reality, for, "*I AM*" or the *awareness of being* is the only reality.

Things live only as long as I am aware of being them; so, to realize one's desire, the second line of this first verse of John must be applied.

That is. *"And the word was with God"* [John 1:1].

The word, or desire, must be fixed or united with consciousness to give it reality.

The awareness becomes aware of *being* the thing desired, thereby nailing itself upon the form or conception—and giving life unto its conception—or resurrecting that which was heretofore a dead or unfulfilled desire.

"Two shall agree as touching anything and it shall be established on earth" [Matt. 18:19].

This agreement is never made between two persons.

It is between the *awareness* and the thing desired.

You are now conscious of *being*, so you are actually saying to yourself, without using words, *"I AM"*.

Now, if it is a state of health that you are desirous of attaining, before you have any evidence of health in your world, you begin to FEEL yourself to be healthy.

And the very second the feeling *"I AM healthy"* is attained, the two have agreed.

That is, *I AM* and *health* have agreed to be one and this agreement ever results in the birth of a child which is the thing agreed upon—in this case, health.

And because I made the agreement, I express the thing agreed.

So you can see why Moses stated, *"I AM hath sent me"* [Exod. 3:14]. For what being, other than *I AM*, could send you into expression?

None—for *"I AM the way—Beside me there is no other"* [Isa. 44:6, 45:5,6].

If you take the wings of the morning and fly into the uttermost parts of the world, or if you make your bed in Hell, you will still be *aware of being*.

You are ever sent into expression by your awareness and your expression is ever that which you are aware of being.

Again, Moses stated, *"I AM that I AM"* [Exod. 3:14].

Now here is something to always bear in mind. *You cannot put new wine in old bottles or new patches upon old garments* [Matt. 9:16,17; Mark 2:21, 22; Luke 5:36–39].

That is, you cannot take with you into the new consciousness any part of the old man.

All of your present beliefs, fears and limitations are weights that bind you to your present level of consciousness.

If you would transcend this level, you must leave behind all that is now your present self, or conception of yourself.

To do this, you take your attention away from all that is now your problem or limitation and dwell upon just *being*.

That is, you say silently but *feeling* to yourself, *"I AM"*.

Do not condition this "awareness" as yet.

Just declare yourself to be, and continue to do so, until you are lost in the feeling of just being—faceless and formless.

When this expansion of consciousness is attained, then, within this formless deep of yourself give form to the new conception by FEELING yourself to be THAT which you desire to be.

You will find within this deep of yourself all things to be divinely possible.

Everything in the world which you can conceive of being is to you, within this present formless awareness, a most natural attainment.

The invitation given us in the Scriptures is—*"to be absent from the body and be present with the Lord"* [2 Cor. 5:8; 1 Cor. 5:3; Col. 2:5].

The "body" being your former conception of yourself and "the Lord"—your *awareness of being.*

This is what is meant when Jesus said to Nicodemus. "*Ye must be born again, for, except ye be born again, ye cannot enter the Kingdom of Heaven*" [John 3:3–7].

That is, except you leave behind you your present conception of yourself and assume the nature of the new birth, you will continue to out-picture your present limitations.

The only way to change your expressions of life is to change your consciousness.

For consciousness is the reality that eternally solidifies itself in the things round about you.

Man's world in its every detail is his consciousness out-pictured.

You can no more change your environment, or world, by destroying *things* than you can your reflection by destroying the mirror.

Your environment, and all within it, reflects that which you are in consciousness.

As long as you continue to be that in consciousness, so long will you continue to out-picture it in your world.

Knowing this, begin to revalue yourself.

Man has placed too little value upon himself.

In the Book of Numbers, you will read, "*In that day there were giants in the land; and we were in our own sight as grasshoppers. And we were in their sight as grasshoppers*" [13:33].

This does not mean a time in the dim past when man had the stature of giants.

Today is the day, the eternal now, when conditions round about you have attained the appearance of giants (such as unemployed, the armies of your enemy, your problems and all things that seem to threaten you); those are the giants that make you feel yourself to be a grasshopper.

But, you are told, you were first, in your own sight a grasshopper and because of this, you were to the giants—a grasshopper.

In other words, you can only be to others what you are first to yourself.

Therefore, to revalue yourself and begin to feel yourself to be the giant, a center of power, is to dwarf these former giants and make of them grasshoppers.

"All the inhabitants of the earth are as nothing, and He doeth according to His will in the armies of Heaven and among all the inhabitants of the earth; and none can stay His hand, nor say unto Him, "What doest Thou?" [Dan. 4:35].

This *being* spoken of is not the orthodox God sitting in space, but the one and only God—the everlasting Father, your *awareness of being.*

So, awake to the power that you are, not as man, but as your true self, a faceless, formless awareness, and free yourself from your self-imposed prison.

"I am the good shepherd and know My sheep and am known of Mine. My sheep hear My voice and I know them and they will follow Me" [John 10:14].

Awareness is the good shepherd.

What I am aware of being is the "sheep that follow me."

So good a "shepherd" is your *awareness* that it has never lost one of the "sheep" that you are aware of being.

I am a voice calling in the wilderness of human confusion for such as I am aware of being, and never shall there come a time when that which I am convinced that I am shall fail to find me.

"I AM" is an open door for all that I am to enter.

Your *awareness of being* is lord and shepherd of your life.

So, *"The Lord is my shepherd; I shall not want"* [Ps. 23:1] is seen in its true light now to be your consciousness.

You could never be in want of proof or lack the evidence of that which you are aware of being.

This being true, why not become aware of being great, God-loving, wealthy, healthy and all attributes that you admire?

It is just as easy to possess the consciousness of these qualities as it is to possess their opposites, for you have not your present consciousness because of your world. On the contrary, your world is what it is because of your present consciousness.

Simple, is it not?

Too simple, in fact, for the wisdom of man that tries to complicate everything.

Paul said of this principle, *"It is to the Greeks"* (or wisdom of this world) *"foolishness"*. *"And to the Jews"* (or those who look for signs) *"a stumbling block"* [1 Cor. 1:23]; with the result that man continues to walk in darkness rather than awake to the being that he is.

Man has so long worshipped the images of his own making, that at first, he finds this revelation blasphemous, since it spells death to all his previous beliefs in a God apart from himself.

This revelation will bring the knowledge that *"I and My Father are one [John 10:30], but My Father is greater than I"* [John 14:28].

You are one with your present conception of yourself.

But you are greater than that which you are at present aware of being.

***Before man can attempt to transform his world, he must first lay the foundation.

—*"I AM the Lord [and there is none else"* [Isa. 45:5].

That is, mans *awareness*, his *consciousness of being is God*.

Until this is firmly established, so that no suggestion or argument put forward by others can shake it, he will find himself returning to the slavery of his former beliefs.***

"If ye believe not that I AM He, ye shall die in your sins" [John 8:24].

That is, you shall continue to be confused and thwarted until you find the cause of your confusion.

When you have lifted up the Son of Man, then shall you know that *I AM* He, that is, that I, John Smith, do nothing of myself, but my father, or *******that state of consciousness which I am now one with does the works.

******* When this is realized, every urge and desire that springs within you shall find expression in your world. *******

"Behold, I stand at the door and knock. If any man hear My voice and open the door, I will come in to him and sup with him and he with Me" [Rev. 3:20].

The *"I"* knocking at the door is the urge. The door is your consciousness.

To open the door is to become one with that that which is knocking by FEELING oneself to *be* the thing desired.

To feel one's desire as impossible is to shut the door or deny this urge expression.

To rise in consciousness to the naturalness of the thing felt is to swing wide the door and invite this one into embodiment.

That is why it is constantly recorded that Jesus left the world of manifestation and ascended unto His Father. Jesus, as you and I, found all things impossible to Jesus, as man.

But having discovered His Father to be the state of consciousness of the thing desired, He but left behind Him the "Jesus consciousness" and rose in consciousness to that state desired and stood upon it until He became one with it.

As He made Himself one with that, He became that in expression.

This is Jesus' simple message to man: Men are but garments that the impersonal being, *I AM*, the presence that men call God—dwells in.

Each garment has certain limitations.

In order to transcend these limitations and give expression to that which, as man—John Smith—you find yourself incapable of doing, you take your attention away from your present limitations, or John Smith conception of yourself, and merge yourself in the feeling of *being* that which you desire.

Just how this desire or newly attained consciousness will embody itself, no man knows.

> *For I, or the newly attained consciousness, has ways that*
> *ye know not of* "I have meat to eat that ye know not of"
> *[John 4:32]; its ways are past finding out [Rom. 11:33].*

Do not speculate as to the HOW of this consciousness embodying itself, for no man is wise enough to know the how.

Speculation is proof that you have not attained to the naturalness of being the thing desired and so are filled with doubts.

You are told, "He who lacks wisdom, let him ask of God, That gives to all liberally, and upbraideth not; and it shall be given unto him.

But let him ask not doubting, for he who doubts is as a wave of the sea that is tossed and battered by the winds. And let not such a one think that he shall receive anything from the Lord" [James 1:5–7].

You can see why this statement is made, for only upon the rock of faith can anything be established.

If you have not the consciousness of the thing, you have not the cause or foundation upon which the thing is erected.

A proof of this established consciousness is given you in the words, *"Thank You, Father"* [*"I thank Thee, O Father, Lord of heaven and earth"* (Matt. 11:25); *"Father, I thank thee that thou hast heard me"* (John 11:41)*].

When you come into the joy of thanksgiving so that you actually feel grateful for having received that which is not yet apparent to the senses, you have definitely become one in consciousness with the thing for which you gave thanks.

God (your *awareness*) is not mocked.

You are ever receiving that which you are aware of being and no man gives thanks for something which he has not received.

"Thank You, Father" is not, as it is used by many today, a sort of magical formula.

You need never utter aloud the words, "Thank You, Father".

In applying this principle, as you rise in consciousness to the point where you are really grateful and happy for having received the thing desired, you automatically rejoice and give thanks inwardly.

You have already accepted the gift which was but a desire before you rose in consciousness, *and your faith is now the substance that shall clothe your desire.*

This rising in consciousness is the spiritual marriage where two shall agree upon being one and *their likeness or image is established on earth [*"if two of you shall agree on earth as touching* *anything that they shall ask, it shall be done for them of My Father which is in heaven"* (Matt. 18:19)*]*.

"For whatsoever ye ask in My Name, the same give I unto you".

["Verily, verily, I say unto you, Whatsoever ye shall ask the Father in My Name, He will give it you" (John 16:23); *"That whatsoever ye shall ask of the Father in My Name, He may give it you"* (John 15:16)*]*.

"Whatsoever" is quite a large measure. It is the unconditional.

It does not state if society deems it right or wrong that you should ask it, it rests with you.

Do you really want it? Do you desire it?

That is all that is necessary. Life will give it to you if you ask "in His Name".

His Name is not a name that you pronounce with the lips. You can ask forever in the name of God or Jehovah or Christ Jesus and you will ask in vain.

"Name means nature; so, when you ask in the nature of a thing, results ever follow".

To ask *in the name* is to rise *[the]* "I" consciousness and become one in nature with the thing desired, rise in consciousness to the nature of the thing, and you will become that thing in expression.

Therefore, "what things soever ye desire, when ye pray, believe that ye receive them and ye shall receive them" [Mark 11:24].

Praying, as we have shown you before, is recognition—the injunction to believe that ye receive is first person, present tense.

This means that you must be in the nature of the things asked for, before you can receive them.

To get into the nature easily, *general amnesty* is necessary.

We are told, *"Forgive, if ye have aught against any, that your Father also, Which is in Heaven, may forgive you. But if ye forgive not, neither will your Father forgive you"* [Mark 11:25.26].

This may seem to be some personal God who is pleased or displeased with your actions but this is not the case.

Consciousness, being God, if you hold in consciousness anything against man, you are binding that condition in your world.

But to release man from all condemnation is to free yourself so that you may rise to any level necessary; there is, therefore, no condemnation to those in Christ Jesus.

Therefore, a very good practice before you enter into your meditation is first to free every man in the world from blame.

For LAW is never violated and you can rest confidently in the knowledge that every man's conception of himself is going to be his reward.

So you do not have to bother yourself about seeing whether or not man gets what you consider he should get.

For life makes no mistakes and always gives man that which man first gives himself.

This brings us to that much abused statement of the Bible on tithing. Teachers of all kinds have enslaved man with this affair of tithing, for not themselves understanding the nature of tithing and being themselves fearful of lack, they have led their followers to believe that a tenth part of their income should be given to the Lord.

Meaning, as they make very clear that, when one gives a tenth part of his income to their particular organization, he is giving his "tenth part" to the Lord—(or is tithing).

But remember, "*I AM* the Lord". Your *awareness of being* is the God that you give to and you ever give in this manner.

Therefore, when you claim yourself to be anything, you have given that claim or quality to God.

And your *awareness of being,* which is no respecter of persons [Acts 10:34; Rom. 2:11], will return to you pressed down, shaken together, and running over with that quality or attribute which you claim for yourself.

Awareness of being is nothing that you could ever name.

To claim God to be rich, to be great, to be love, to be all wise, is to define that which cannot be defined.

For God is nothing that could ever be named.

Tithing is necessary and you do tithe with God.

But from now on give to the only God and see to it that you give him the quality that you desire as man to express *by claiming yourself to be the great, the wealthy, the loving, the allwise.*

Do not speculate as to how you shall express these qualities or claims, for life has a way that you, as man, know not of. Its ways are past finding out.

But, I assure you, the day you claim these qualities to the point of conviction, your claims will be honored.

There is nothing covered that shall *[not]* be uncovered *["There is nothing covered, that shall not be revealed; and hid, that shall not be known" (Matt. 10:26); "There is nothing covered, that shall not be revealed; neither hid, that shall not be known" (Luke 12:2)].*

That which is spoken in secret shall be proclaimed from the housetops *["What I tell you in darkness, that speak ye in light: and what ye hear in the ear, that preach ye upon the housetops" (Matt. 10:27); "Whatsoever ye have spoken in darkness shall be*

*heard in the light; and that which ye have spoken in the ear in clos-
ets shall be proclaimed upon the housetops"* (Luke 12:3)*]*.

That is, your secret convictions of yourself—these secret claims that no man knows of, when really believed, will be shouted from the housetops in your world.

For your convictions of yourself are the words of the God within you, which words are spirit and cannot return unto you void, but must accomplish whereunto they are sent *["So shall My word be that goeth forth out of My mouth: it shall not return unto Me void, but it shall accomplish that which I please, and it shall prosper in the thing whereto I sent it"* (Isa. 55:11)*]*.

You are at this moment calling out of the infinite that which you are now conscious of being.

And not one word or conviction will fail to find you.

"I AM the vine and ye are the branches" [John 15:5]. Consciousness is the "vine" and those qualities which you are now conscious of being are as "branches" that you feed and keep alive.

Just as a branch has no life except it be rooted in the vine, so likewise things have no life except you be conscious of them.

Just as a branch withers and dies if the sap of the vine ceases to flow towards it, so do things in your world pass away if you take your attention from them, because your attention is as the sap of life that keeps alive and sustains the things of your world.

To dissolve a problem that now seems so real to you, all that you do is remove your attention from it. In spite of its seeming reality, turn from it in consciousness.

Become indifferent and begin to feel yourself to be that which would be the solution of the problem.

For instance, if you were imprisoned, no man would have

to tell you that you should desire freedom. Freedom, or rather the desire of freedom would be automatic.

So why look behind the four walls of your prison bars? Take your attention from being imprisoned and begin to feel yourself to be free. FEEL it to the point where it is natural—the very second you do so, those prison bars will dissolve. Apply this same principle to any problem.

I have seen people who were in debt up to their ears apply this principle and in the twinkling of an eye, debts that were mountainous were removed. I have seen those whom doctors had given up as incurable take their attention away from their problem of disease and begin to feel themselves to be well in spite of the evidence of their sense to the contrary. In no time at all, this so-called "incurable disease" vanished and left no scar.

Your answer to, *"Whom do you say that I AM"?* [Matt. 16:15; Mark 8:29; Luke 9:20] ever determines your expression.

As long as you are conscious of being imprisoned or diseased or poor, so long will you continue to out-picture or express these conditions.

When man realized that he *is* now *that* which he is seeking and begins to claim that he is, he will have the proof of his claim.

This cue is given you in words. *"Whom seek ye?"* [John 18:4, 18:7]. And they answered, "Jesus". And the voice said, "I *am* He".

"Jesus" here means salvation or savior.

You are seeking to be salvaged from that which is not your problem.

"I am" is He that will save you.

If you are hungry, your savior is food.

If you are poor, your savior is riches.

If you are imprisoned, your savior is freedom.

If you are diseased, it will not be a man called Jesus who will save you, but health will become your savior.

Therefore, claim "I am He", in other words, claim yourself to be the thing desired.

Claim it in consciousness—not in words—and consciousness will reward you with your claim.

You are told, "You shall find Me when you FEEL after Me" *["And ye shall seek Me, and find Me, when ye shall search for Me with all your heart"* (Jer. 29:13)].

Well, FEEL after that quality in consciousness until you FEEL yourself to be it. When you lose yourself in the feeling of being it, the quality will embody itself in your world.

You are healed from your problem when you touch the solution of it.

"Who has touched Me? For I perceive virtue is gone out of Me" *[Luke 8:46: "And Jesus, immediately knowing in Himself that virtue had gone out of Him, turned Him about in the press, and said, "Who touched My clothes?"* (Mark 5:30)].

Yes, the day you touch this being within you—FEELING yourself to be cured or healed, virtues will come out of your very self and solidify themselves in your world as healings.

It is said, *"You believe in God. Believe also in Me, for I am He"* [John 14:1].

Have the faith of God. *"He made Himself one with God and found it not robbery to do the works of God"* [Phil. 2:6].

Go you and do likewise. Yes, begin to believe your *awareness,* your *consciousness of being* to be God.

Claim for yourself all the attributes that you have heretofore given an external God and you will begin to express these claims.

"For I am not a God afar off" [William Blake, "Jerusalem", 4:19]. *I am nearer than your hands and feet—nearer than your very breathing.*

I am your *awareness of being.*

I am that in which all that I shall ever be *aware of being* shall begin and end.

"For before the world was, I AM; and when the world shall cease to be, I AM" [Adon Olam, Jewish dogmatics]; *"before Abraham was, I AM"* [John 8:58].

This *I AM* is your *awareness.*

[He was in the world, and the world was made by Him, and the world knew Him not (John 1:10); With the glory which I had with Thee before the world was (John 17:5); My glory, which You gave Me because You loved Me before the world was made (John 17:24); The wisdom of God in a mystery, even the hidden wisdom, which God ordained before the world unto our glory (1 Cor. 2:7); He hath chosen us in Him before the foundation of the world (Eph. 1:4); According to his own purpose and grace, which was given us in Christ Jesus before the world began (2 Tim. 1:9); Who verily was foreordained before the foundation of the world (1 Pet. 1:20)].

"Except the Lord build the house, they labor in vain that build it" [Ps. 127:1].

"The Lord" being your consciousness, except that which you seek is first established in your consciousness, you will labor in vain to find it.

All things must begin and end in consciousness.

So, blessed indeed is the man that trusteth in himself ["Blessed is the man that trusteth in the LORD, and whose hope the LORD is" (Jer. 17:7); "O LORD of hosts, blessed is the man that trusteth in Thee" (Ps. 84:12)]—for man's faith in God will *ever be measured by his confidence in himself. You believe in God, believe also in ME* [John 14:1].

Put not your trust in men [*"Put not your trust in princes, nor in the son of man, in whom there is no help"* (Ps. 146:3)], for men but reflect the being that you are, and can only bring to you or do unto you that which you have first done unto yourself.

"No man taketh away My life, I lay it down Myself. I have the power to lay it down and the power to take it up again" [John 10:18].

No matter what happens to man in this world, it is never an accident. It occurs under the guidance of an exact and changeless Law.

"No man" (manifestation) *"comes unto Me, except the Father within Me draw him"* [John 6:44] and *"I and My father are One"* [John 10:30].

Believe this truth and you will be free. Man has always blamed others for that which he is and will continue to do so until he find himself as cause of all.

"I AM" comes not to destroy, but to fulfill.

"I AM", the awareness *within you, destroys nothing but ever fills full the molds or conception one has of one's self.*

It is impossible for the poor man to find wealth in this world, no matter how he is surrounded with it. ***until he first claims himself to be wealthy.***

For signs follow, they do not precede.

To constantly kick and complain against the limitations of poverty, while remaining poor in consciousness, is to play the fool's game.

Changes cannot take place from that level of consciousness, for life is constantly out-picturing all levels.

Follow the example of the prodigal son [Luke 15:11–32].

Realize that you, yourself, brought about this condition of waste and lack and make the decision within yourself to rise to a higher level, where the fatted calf, the ring and the robe await your claim.

There was no condemnation of the prodigal when he had the courage to claim this inheritance as his own.

Others will condemn us only as long as we continue in that for which we condemn ourselves.

So: *"Happy is the man that condemneth himself not in that which he alloweth"* [Rom. 14:22]. For to life, nothing is condemned. All is expressed.

Life does not care whether you call yourself rich or poor; strong or weak.

It will eternally reward you with that which you claim as true of yourself.

The measurements of right and wrong belong to man alone. To life, there is nothing right or wrong. As Paul stated in his letters to the Romans: *"I know and am persuaded by the Lord Jesus that there is nothing unclean of itself but to him that esteemeth anything to be unclean, to him it is unclean"* [14:14].

Stop asking yourself whether you are worthy or unworthy to receive that which you desire. You, as man, did not create the desire.

Your desires are ever fashioned within you because of what you now claim yourself to be.

When a man is hungry, (without thinking) he automatically desires food. When imprisoned, he automatically desires freedom and so forth.

Your desires contain within themselves the plan of self-expression.

So leave all judgments out of the picture and rise in consciousness to the level of your desire and make yourself one with it by claiming it to be so now.

For: *"My grace is sufficient for thee. My strength is made perfect in weakness"* [2 Cor. 12:9].

Have faith in this unseen claim until the conviction is born within you that it is so.

Your confidence in this claim will pay great rewards.

Just a little while and he, the thing desired, will come.

But without faith, it is impossible to realize anything.

Through faith, the worlds were framed, because *"faith is the substance of the thing hoped for—the evidence of the thing not yet seen"* [Heb. 11:1].

Don't be anxious or concerned as to results. They will follow just as surely as day follows night.

Look upon your desires—all of them—as the spoken words of God, and every word or desire a promise.

The reason most of us fail to realize our desires is because we are constantly conditioning them.

Do not condition your desire.

Just accept it as it comes to you.

Give thanks for it to the point that you are grateful for having already received it—then go about your way in peace.

Such acceptance of your desire is like dropping seed—fertile seed—into prepared soil.

For when you can drop the thing desired in consciousness, confident that it shall appear, you have done all that is expected to you.

But, to be worried or concerned about the HOW of your desire maturing is to hold these fertile seeds in a mental grasp, and, therefore, never to have dropped them in the soil of confidence.

The reason men condition their desires is because they constantly judge after the appearance of being and see the things as real—forgetting that the only reality is the consciousness back of them.

To see things as real is to deny that all things are possible to God *["With men this is impossible: but with God all things are possible"* (Matt. 19:26); *"With men it is impossible, but not with God: for with God all things are possible"* (Mark 10:27)].

The man who is imprisoned and sees his four walls as real is automatically denying the urge or promise of God within him of freedom.

A question often asked when this statement is made is, if one's desire is a gift of God, how can you say that if one desires to kill a man that such a desire is good and therefore God sent? In answer to this, let me say that no man desires to kill another. What he does desire is to be freed from such a one. But because he does not believe that the desire to be free from such a one contains within itself the powers of freedom, he conditions that desire and sees the only way to express such freedom is to destroy the man—forgetting that the life wrapped within the desire has ways that he, as man, knows not of.

Its ways are past finding out.

Thus, man distorts the gifts of God through his lack of faith.

Problems are the mountains spoken of that can be removed if one has but the faith of a grain of a mustard seed.

Men approach their problem as did the old lady who, on attending service and hearing the priest say, "If you had but the faith of a grain of a mustard seed, you would say unto yonder mountain 'be thou removed' and it shall be removed and nothing is impossible to you" [Matt. 17:20] *["If ye had faith as a grain of mustard seed, ye might say unto this sycamine tree. Be thou plucked up by the root, and be thou planted in the sea; and it should obey you"* (Luke 17:6)*]*.

That night, as she said her prayers, she quoted this part of the scriptures and retired to bed in what she thought was faith. On arising in the morning, she rushed to the window and exclaimed: "I knew that old mountain would still be there".

For this is how man approaches his problems. He knows that they are still going to confront him. And because life is no respecter of persons [Acts 10:34; Rom. 2:11] and destroys nothing, it continues to keep alive that which he is conscious of being.

Things will disappear only as man changes in consciousness.

Deny it if you will, it still remains a fact that consciousness is the only reality and things but mirror that which you are in consciousness.

So the heavenly state you are seeking will be found only in consciousness, *"for the Kingdom of Heaven is within you"* [Luke 17:21].

As the will of heaven is ever done on earth, you are today living in the heaven that you have established within you.

For here, on this very earth, your heaven reveals itself. The Kingdom of Heaven really is at hand.

NOW is the accepted time.

So create a new heaven, enter into a new state of consciousness and a new earth will appear.

"The former things shall pass away" [Rev. 21:4]. They shall not be remembered, not come into mind any more. *"For, behold, I"* (your consciousness) *"come quickly and My reward is with Me"* [Rev. 22:12].

I am nameless, but will take upon Myself every name (nature) that you call Me. Remember, it is you, yourself, that I speak of as "me".

So every conception that you have of yourself—that is every deep conviction you have of yourself—is that which you shall appear as being; for *I AM [is]* not fooled: God is not mocked.

Now let me instruct you in the art of fishing.

It is recorded that the disciples fished all night and caught nothing. Then Jesus came upon the scene and told them to cast their nets in once more, into the same waters that only a moment before were barren—and this time their nets were bursting with the catch [John 21:3–6].

This story is taking place in the world today right within you, the reader. For you have within you all the elements necessary to go fishing.

But until you find that Jesus Christ (your awareness) is Lord, you will fish, as did these disciples, in the night of human darkness.

That is, you will fish for THINGS thinking things to be real and will fish with the human bait—which is a struggle and an effort—trying to make contact with this one and that one: trying to coerce this being or the other being; and all such effort will be in vain.

But when you discover your *awareness of being* to be Christ Jesus, you will let Him direct your fishing.

And you will fish in consciousness for the things that you desire.

For your desire will be the fish that you will catch, because your consciousness is the only living reality you will fish in the deep waters of consciousness.

If you would catch that which is beyond your present capacity, you must launch out into deeper waters, for, within your present consciousness, such fish or desires cannot swim.

To launch out into deeper waters, you leave behind you all that is now your present problem, or limitation, by taking your ATTENTION AWAY from it.

Turn your back completely upon every problem and limitation that you now possess. Dwell upon just *being* by saying. "*I AM*", "*I AM*", "*I AM*" to yourself.

Continue to declare to yourself that you just *are*.

Do not condition this declaration, just continue to FEEL yourself to *be* and without warning you will find yourself slipping the anchor that tied you to the shallow of your problems and moving out into the deep.

This is usually accompanied with the feeling of expansion.

You will FEEL yourself expand as though you were actually growing. Don't be afraid, for courage is necessary.

You are not going to die to anything but your former limitations, but they are going to die as you move away from them, for they live only in your consciousness.

In this deep or expanded consciousness you will find yourself to be a power that you had never dreamt of before.

The things desired before you shoved off from the shores of limitation are the fish you are going to catch in this deep.

Because you have lost all consciousness of your problems and barriers, it is now the easiest thing in the world to FEEL yourself to be one with the things desired.

Because *I AM* (your consciousness) is the resurrection and the life, you must attach this resurrecting power that you are to the thing desired if you would make it appear and live in your world.

Now you begin to assume the nature of the thing desired by feeling, "*I AM* wealthy"; "*I AM* free"; "*I AM* strong".

When these "FEELS" are fixed within yourself, your formless being will take upon itself the forms of the things felt. You become "crucified" upon the feelings of wealth, freedom and strength.

Remain buried in the stillness of these convictions. Then, as a thief in the night and when you least expect it, these qualities will be resurrected in your world as living realities.

The world shall touch you and see that you are flesh and blood, for you shall begin to bear fruit of the nature of these qualities newly appropriated.

This is the art of successful fishing for the manifestations of life.

Successful realization of the thing desired is also told us in the story of Daniel in the lions' den [Dan. 6:16–23]. Here, it is recorded that Daniel, while in the lions' den, turned his back upon the lions and looked towards the light coming from above; that the lions remained powerless and Daniel's faith in his God saved him.

This also is your story and you too must do as Daniel did.

If you found yourself in a lions' den, you would have no other concern but lions. You would not be thinking of one thing in the world but your problem—which problem would be lions.

Yet, you are told that Daniel turned his back upon them and looked towards the light that was his God.

If we would follow the example of Daniel, we would, while imprisoned within the den of poverty or sickness, take our attention away from our problems of debts or sickness and dwell upon the thing we seek.

If we do not look back in consciousness to our problems, but continue in faith—believing ourselves to be that which we seek—, we too will find our prison walls open and the thing sought—yes, "whatsoever things" [John 16:23]—realized.

Another story is told us; of the widow and the three drops of oil [2 Kings 4:1–6]. The prophet [Elisha] asked the widow, "What have ye in your house?" And she replied, "Three drops of oil".

He then said to her, "Go borrow vessels. Close the door after ye have returned into your house and begin to pour". And she poured from three drops of oil into all the borrowed vessels, filling them to capacity with oil remaining.

You, the reader, are this widow.

You have not a husband to impregnate you or make you fruitful, for a "widow" is a barren state.

Your *awareness* is now the Lord—or the prophet that has become your husband.

Follow the example of the widow, who instead of recognizing an emptiness or nothingness, recognized the something—three drops of oil.

Then, the command to her. *"Go within and close the door"*, that is, shut the door of the senses that tell you of the empty measures, the debts, the problems.

When you have taken your attention away completely by shutting out the evidence of the senses, begin to FEEL the joy (symbolized by oil)—of having received the things desired.

When the agreement is established within you so that all doubts and fears have passed away, then, you too will fill all the empty measures of your life and will have an abundance running over.

Recognition is the power that conjures in the world.

Every state that you have ever recognized, you have embodied.

That which you are recognizing as true of yourself today is that which you are experiencing.

So be as the widow and recognize joy, no matter how little the beginnings of recognition, and you will be generously rewarded—for the world is a magnified mirror, magnifying everything that you are conscious of being.

"I AM the Lord thy God, which has brought thee out of the land of Egypt, out of the house of bondage; thou shalt have not other gods before Me" [Exod. 20:2.3].

What a glorious revelation, your *awareness* now revealed as the Lord thy God!

Come, awake from your dream of being imprisoned.

Realize that the earth is yours, "and the fullness thereof; the world and all that dwells therein" [Ps. 24:1].

You have become so enmeshed in the belief that you are man, that you have forgotten the glorious being that you are.

Now, with your memory restored, DECREE the unseen to appear and it SHALL appear, for all things are compelled to respond to the Voice of God, Your *awareness of being*—the world is *AT YOUR COMMAND!*

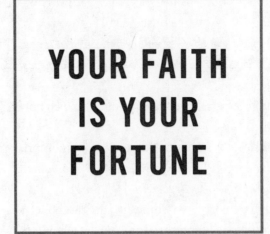

YOUR FAITH
IS YOUR
FORTUNE

YOUR FAITH IS YOUR FORTUNE

by

Neville

1941

Man's faith in god is measured by his confidence in himself

CONTENTS

BEFORE ABRAHAM WAS

Verily, verily, I say unto you, before Abraham was, I AM.

—JOHN 8:58

"In the beginning was the Word, and the Word was with God, and the Word was God" [John 1:1].

In the beginning was the unconditioned awareness of being, and the unconditioned awareness of being became conditioned by imagining itself to be something, and the unconditioned awareness of being became that which it had imagined itself to be; so did creation begin.

By this law—first conceiving, then becoming that conceived—all things evolve out of Nothing; and without this sequence there is not anything made that is made.

Before Abraham or the world was—I AM. When all of time shall cease to be—I AM. I AM the formless awareness of being conceiving myself to be man. By my everlasting law of being I am compelled to be and to express all that I believe myself to be.

I AM the eternal No-thingness containing within my formless self the capacity to be all things.

I AM that in which all my conceptions of myself live and move and have their being, and apart from which they are not.

I dwell within every conception of myself; from this within-inness, I ever seek to transcend all conceptions of myself. By the very law of my being, I transcend my conceptions of myself, only as I believe myself to be that which does transcend.

I AM the law of being and beside ME there is no law. I AM that I AM.

] 2 [

YOU SHALL DECREE

[Thou shalt also decree a thing and it shall be established unto thee and the light shall shine upon thy ways. You will also decree a thing, and it will be established for you; And light will shine on your ways. Thou shalt decree a thing, and it I shall come to thee, and light shall shine in thy ways.]

—Job 22:28

So shall My word be that goeth forth out of My mouth; it shall not return unto Me void, but it shall accomplish that which I please, and it shall prosper in the thing whereto I sent it.

—Isaiah 55:11

Man can decree a thing and it will come to pass.

Man has always decreed that which has appeared in his world. He is today decreeing that which is appearing in his world and he shall continue to do so as long as man is conscious of being man.

Nothing has ever appeared in man's world, but what man decreed that it should. This you may deny; but try as you will, you cannot disprove it for this decreeing is based upon a changeless principle.

Man does not command things to appear by his words, which are, more often than not, a confession of his doubts and fears.

Decreeing is ever done in consciousness.

Every man automatically expresses that which he is conscious of being. Without effort or the use of words, at every moment of time, man is commanding himself to be and to possess that which he is conscious of being and possessing.

This changeless principle of expression is dramatized in all the Bibles of the world. The writers of our sacred books were illumined mystics, past masters in the art of psychology. In telling the story of the soul, they personified this impersonal principle in the form of a historical document both to preserve it and to hide it from the eyes of the uninitiated.

Today, those to whom this great treasure has been entrusted, namely, the priesthoods of the world, have forgotten that the Bibles are psychological dramas representing the consciousness of man; in their blind forgetfulness, they now teach their followers to worship its characters as men and women who actually lived in time and space.

When man sees the Bible as a great psychological drama, with all of its characters and actors as the personified qualities and attributes of his own consciousness, then—and then only—will the Bible reveal to him the light of its symbology.

This Impersonal principle of life which made all things is personified as God.

This Lord God, creator of heaven and earth, is discovered to be man's awareness of being.

If man were less bound by orthodoxy and more intuitively

observant, he could not fail to notice in the reading of the Bibles that the awareness of being is revealed hundreds of times throughout this literature.

To name a few: "I AM hath sent me unto you" [Exod. 3:14]. "Be still and know that I AM God" [Ps. 46:10]. "I AM the Lord and there is no other God" ["*I am the LORD, and there is none else, there is no God beside Me*" (Isa. 45:5); "*I am the LORD your God, And there is no other*" (Joel 2:27)]. "I AM the shepherd" ["*I am the good shepherd: the good shepherd giveth His life for the sheep*" (John 10:11); "*I am the good shepherd, and know My sheep, and am known of Mine*" (John 10:14)]. "I AM the door" ["*I am the door: by Me if any man enter in, he shall be saved, and shall go in and out, and find pasture*" (John 10:9); "*Verily, verily, I say unto you, I am the door of the sheep*" (John 10:7)]. "I AM the resurrection and the life" [John 11:25]. "I AM the way" ["*I am the* way, *and the truth, and the life; no one cometh to the Father but through Me*" (John 14:6)]. "I AM the beginning and the end" ["*I am Alpha and Omega, the beginning and the end, the first and the last*" (Rev. 22:13); "*I am Alpha and Omega, the beginning and the ending, saith the Lord, Which is, and Which was, and Which is to come, the Almighty*" (Rev. 1:8)].

I AM; man's unconditioned awareness of being is revealed as Lord and Creator of every conditioned state of being.

If man would give up his belief in a God apart from himself, recognize his awareness of being to be God (this awareness fashions itself in the likeness and image of its conception of itself), he would transform his world from a barren waste to a fertile field of his own liking.

The day man does this he will know that he and his Father are one, but his Father is greater than he. He will know that his consciousness of being is one with that which he is conscious of being, but that his unconditioned consciousness of being is greater than his conditioned state or his conception of himself.

When man discovers his consciousness to be the impersonal power of expression, which power eternally personifies itself in his conceptions of himself, he will assume and appropriate that state of consciousness which he desires to express; in so doing he will become that state in expression.

"Ye shall decree a thing and it shall come to pass" can now be told in this manner: You shall become conscious of being or possessing a thing and you shall express or possess that which you are conscious of being.

The law of consciousness is the only law of expression.

"I AM the way". "I AM the resurrection".

Consciousness is the way as well as the power which resurrects and expresses all that man will ever be conscious of being.

Turn from the blindness of the uninitiated man who attempts to express and possess those qualities and things which he is not conscious of being and possessing; and be as the illumined mystic who decrees on the basis of this changeless law. Consciously claim yourself to be that which you seek; appropriate the consciousness of that which you see; and you too will know the status of the true mystic, as follows:

I became conscious of being it. I am still conscious of being it. And I shall continue to be conscious of being it until that which I am conscious of being is perfectly expressed.

Yes, I shall decree a thing and it shall come to pass.

] 3 [

THE PRINCIPLE OF TRUTH

Ye shall know the truth, and the truth shall make you free.
— JOHN 8:32

"Ye shall know the truth and the truth shall set you free".
The truth that sets man free is the knowledge that his consciousness is the resurrection and the life, that his consciousness both resurrects and makes alive all that he is conscious of being.

Apart from consciousness, there is neither resurrection nor life.

When man gives up his belief in a God apart from himself and begins to recognize his awareness of being to be God, as did Jesus and the prophets, he will transform his world with the realization, *"I and My Father are one"* [John 10:30], but *"My Father is greater than I"* [John 14:28].

He will know that his consciousness is God and that which he is conscious of being is the Son bearing witness of God, the Father.

The conceiver and the conception are one, but the conceiver

is greater than his conception. Before Abraham was, I AM. Yes, I was aware of being before I became aware of being man, and in that day when I shall cease to be conscious of being man I shall still be conscious of being.

The consciousness of being is not dependent upon being anything.

It preceded all conceptions of itself and shall be when all conceptions of itself shall cease to be. "I AM the beginning and the end". That is, all things or conceptions of myself begin and end in me, but I, the formless awareness, remain forever.

Jesus discovered this glorious truth and declared Himself to be one with God, not the God that man had fashioned, for He never recognized such a God.

Jesus found God to be His awareness of being and so told man that the Kingdom of God and Heaven were within [Luke 17:21,23].

When it is recorded that Jesus left the world and went to His Father ["He was received up into heaven" (Mark 16:19; Luke 24:51)], it is simply stating that He turned His attention from the world of the senses and rose in consciousness to that level which He desired to express.

There He remained until He became one with the consciousness to which He ascended. When He returned to the world of man, He could act with the positive assurance of that which He was conscious of being, a state of consciousness no one but Himself felt or knew that He possessed.

Man who is ignorant of this everlasting law of expression looks upon such happenings as miracles.

To rise in consciousness to the level of the thing desired and to remain there until such level becomes your nature is the way of all seeming miracles. "And I, if I be lifted up, I shall draw all men unto Me" [*And I, if I be lifted up from the earth, will draw all men unto Me*" (John 12:32)]. If I be lifted up in consciousness to the naturalness of the thing desired. I shall draw the manifestation of that desire to me.

"*No man comes unto Me save the Father within Me draws him*" [John 6:44], and "*I and My Father are one*" [John 10:30].

My consciousness is the Father who draws the manifestation of life to me. The nature of the manifestation is determined by the state of consciousness in which I dwell. I am always drawing into my world that which I am conscious of being.

If you are dissatisfied with your present expression of life, then you must be born again [John 3:7]. Rebirth is the dropping of that level with which you are dissatisfied and rising to that level of consciousness which you desire to express and possess.

You cannot serve two masters [Matt. 6:24; Luke 16:13] or opposing states of consciousness at the same time.

Taking your attention from one state and placing it upon the other, you die to the one from which you have taken it and you live and express the one with which you are united.

Man cannot see how it would be possible to express that which he desires to be by so simple a law as acquiring the consciousness of the thing desired.

The reason for this lack of faith on the part of man is that he looks at the desired state through the consciousness of his present limitations. Therefore, he naturally sees it as impossible of accomplishment.

One of the first things man must realize is that it is impossible, in dealing with this spiritual law of consciousness, to put new wine into old bottles or new patches on old garments [Matt. 9:16, 17; Mark 2:21,22; Luke 5:36–39].

That is, you cannot take any part of the present conscious-ness into the new state. For the state sought is complete in itself and needs no patching. Every level of consciousness au-tomatically expresses itself.

To rise to the level of any state is to automatically become that state in expression. But, in order to rise to the level that you are not now expressing, you must completely drop the consciousness with which you are now identified.

Until your present consciousness is dropped, you will not be able to rise to another level.

Do not be dismayed. This letting go of your present iden-tity is not as difficult as it might appear to be.

The invitation of the scriptures, *"To be absent from the body and be present with the Lord"* [2 Cor. 5:8; 1 Cor. 5:3; Col. 2:5], is not given to a select few; it is a sweeping call to all man-kind. The body from which you are invited to escape is your present conception of yourself with all of its limitations, while the Lord with whom you are to be present is your awareness of being.

To accomplish this seemingly impossible feat, you take your attention away from your problem and place it upon just being. You say silently but feelingly, "I AM". Do not condi-tion this awareness but continue declaring quietly, "I AM—I AM". Simply feel that you are faceless and formless and con-tinue doing so until you feel yourself floating.

"Floating" is a psychological state which completely denies the physical. Through practice in relaxation and willfully re-fusing to react to sensory impressions, it is possible to develop a state of consciousness of pure receptivity. It is a surprisingly easy accomplishment. In this state of complete detachment, a definite singleness of purposeful thought can be indelibly engraved upon your unmodified consciousness. This state of consciousness is necessary for true meditation.

This wonderful experience of rising and floating is the signal that you are absent from the body or problem and are now present with the Lord; in this expanded state you are not conscious of being anything but I AM—I AM; you are only conscious of being.

When this expansion of consciousness is attained, within this formless deep of yourself, give form to the new conception by claiming and feeling yourself to be that which you, before you entered into this state, desired to be. You will find that within this formless deep of yourself all things appear to be divinely possible. Anything that you sincerely feel yourself to be while in this expanded state becomes, in time, your natural expression.

And God said, "Let there be a firmament in the midst of the waters" [Gen. 1:6]. Yes, let there be a firmness or conviction in the midst of this expanded consciousness by knowing and feeling I AM that, the thing desired.

As you claim and feel yourself to be the thing desired, you are crystallizing this formless liquid light that you are into the image and likeness [Gen. 1:26] of that which you are conscious of being.

Now that the law of your being has been revealed to you, begin this day to change your world by revaluing yourself. Too long has man held to the belief that he is born of sorrow and must work out his salvation by the sweat of his brow. God is impersonal and no respecter of persons [Acts 10:34; Rom. 2:11]. So long as man continues to walk in this belief of sorrow, so long will he walk. In a world of sorrow and confusion, for the world in its every detail is man's consciousness crystallized.

In the Book of Numbers it is recorded, *"There were giants in the land and we were in our own sight as grasshoppers, and we were in their sight as grasshoppers"* [13:33].

Today is the day, the eternal now, when conditions in the world have attained the appearance of giants. The unemployed, the armies of the enemy, business competition etc. are the giants which make you feel yourself to be a helpless grasshopper. We are told we were first in our own sight helpless grasshoppers and because of this conception of ourselves were to the enemy helpless grasshoppers.

We can be to others only that which we are to ourselves.

Therefore, as we revalue ourselves and begin to feel ourselves to be the giant, a center of power, we automatically change our relationship to the giants, reducing these former monsters to their true place, making them appear to be the helpless grasshoppers.

Paul said of this principle, "It is to the Greeks (or the so-called wise men of the world) foolishness; and to the Jews (or those who look for signs) a stumbling block" [*"For the Jews require a sign, and the Greeks seek after wisdom: But we preach Christ crucified, unto the Jews a stumbling block, and unto the Greeks foolishness; But unto them which are called, both Jews and Greeks. Christ the power of God, and the wisdom of God. Because the foolishness of God is wiser than men; and the weakness of God is stronger than men"* (1 Cor. 1:22–25]; with the result that man continues to walk in darkness rather than awake to the realization, "I AM the light of the world" [Matt. 5:14; John 8:12].

Man has so long worshipped the images of his own making that at first he finds this revelation blasphemous, but the day man discovers and accepts this principle as the basis of his life, that day man slays his belief in a God apart from himself.

The story of Jesus' betrayal in the Garden of Gethsemane is the perfect illustration of man's discovery of this principle. We are told, the crowds armed with staves and lanterns sought Jesus in the dark of night.

As they inquired after the whereabouts of Jesus (salvation), the voice answered, "I AM"; whereupon the entire crowd fell to the ground. On regaining their composure, they again asked to be shown the hiding place of the savior and again the savior said, *"I have told you that I AM, therefore if ye seek Me, let all else go"* [John 18:8].

Man in the darkness of human ignorance sets out on his search for God, aided by the flickering light of human wisdom.

As it is revealed to man that his I AM or awareness of being is his savior, the shock is so great, he mentally falls to the ground, for every belief that he has ever entertained tumbles as he realizes that his consciousness is the one and only savior.

The knowledge that his I AM is God compels man to let all others go for he finds it impossible to serve two Gods. Man cannot accept his awareness of being as God and at the same time believe in another deity.

With this discovery, man's human ear or hearing (understanding) is cut off by the sword of faith (Peter) as his perfect disciplined hearing (understanding) is restored by (Jesus) the knowledge that I AM is Lord and Savior.

Before man can transform his world, he must first lay this foundation or understanding. *"I AM the Lord [and there is none else"* [Isaiah 45:5].

Man must know that his awareness of being is God.

Until this is firmly established so that no suggestion or argument of others can shake him, he will find himself returning to the slavery of his former belief.

"If ye believe not that I AM He, ye shall die in your sins" [John 8:24].

Unless man discovers that his consciousness is the cause of every expression of his life, he will continue seeking the cause of his confusion in the world of effects, and so shall die in his fruitless search.

"I AM the vine and ye are the branches" [John 15:5].

Consciousness is the vine and that which you are conscious of being is as branches that you feed and keep alive. Just as a branch has no life except it be rooted in the vine, likewise things have no life except you be conscious of them.

Just as a branch withers and dies if the sap of the vine ceases to flow towards it, so do things and qualities pass away if you take your attention from them; because your attention is the sap of life which sustains the expression of your life.

] 4 [

WHOM SEEK YE?

I have told you that I AM; if therefore ye seek Me, let these go their way.

—John 18:8

As soon then as He had said unto them, I AM, they went backward and fell to the ground.

—John 18:6

Today there is so much said about Masters, Elder Brothers, Adepts and initiates that numberless truth seekers are being constantly misled by seeking these false lights.

For a price, most of these pseudo-teachers offer their students initiation into the mysteries, promising them guidance and direction. Man's weakness for leaders, as well as his worship of idols, makes him an easy prey of these schools and teachers.

Good will come to most of these enrolled students; they will discover after years of awaiting and sacrificing that they were following a mirage.

They will then become disillusioned in their schools and teachers, and this disappointment will be worth the effort and price they have paid for their fruitless search.

They will then turn from their worship of man and in so doing discover that which they are seeking is not to be found in another, for *the Kingdom of Heaven is within* [Luke 17:21].

This realization will be their first real initiation.

The lesson learned will be this: There is only one Master and this Master is God, the I AM within themselves.

"I AM the Lord thy God who led thee out of the land of darkness: out of the house of bondage" [Exod. 20:2, Deut. 5:6].

I AM, your awareness, is Lord and Master and besides your awareness there is neither Lord nor Master.

You are Master of all that you will ever be aware of being.

You know that you are, do you not? Knowing that you are is the Lord and Master of that which you know that you are.

You could be completely isolated by man from that which you are conscious of being; yet you would, in spite of all human barriers, effortlessly draw to yourself all that you were conscious of being.

The man who is conscious of being poor does not need the assistance of anyone to express his poverty. The man who is conscious of being sick, though isolated in the most hermetically sealed germ-proof area in the world, would express sickness.

There is no barrier to God, for God is your awareness of being.

Regardless of what you are aware of being, you can and do express it without effort.

Stop looking for the Master to come: he is with you always. *"I AM with you always, even unto the end of the world"* [Matt. 28:20].

You will from time to time know yourself to be many things, but you need not be anything to know that you are.

You can, if you so desire, disentangle yourself from the body you wear; in so doing, you realize that you are a faceless, formless awareness and not dependent on the form you are in your expression.

You will know that you are; you will also discover that this knowing that you are is God, the Father, which preceded all that you ever knew yourself to be.

Before the world was, you were aware of being and so you were saying "I AM", and I AM will be, after all that you know yourself to be shall cease to be.

There are no Ascended Masters. Banish this superstition.

You will forever rise from one level of consciousness (master) to another; in so doing, you manifest the ascended level, expressing this newly acquired consciousness.

Consciousness being Lord and Master, you are the Master Magician conjuring that which you are now conscious of being.

"For God (consciousness) calleth those things which be not as though they were" [Rom. 4:17]: things that are not now seen will be seen the moment you become conscious of being that which is not now seen.

This rising from one level of consciousness to another is the only ascension that you will ever experience.

No man can lift you to the level you desire. The power to ascend is within yourself; it is your consciousness.

You appropriate the consciousness of the level you desire to express by claiming that you are now expressing such a level.

This is the ascension. It is limitless, for you will never exhaust your capacity to ascend.

Turn from the human superstition of ascension with its belief in masters, and find the only and everlasting master within yourself.

"Far greater is he that is in you than he that is in the world" [1 John 4:4]. Believe this.

Do not continue in blindness, following after the mirage of masters. I assure you your search can end only in disappointment.

"If you deny Me (your awareness of being), I shall deny you also" [Matt. 10:33]. "Thou shalt have no other God beside ME" [Isa. 45:5; Joel 2:27]. "Be still and know that I AM God" [Ps. 46:10]. "Come prove me and see if I will not open you the windows of Heaven and pour you out a blessing, that there shall not be room enough to receive it" [Mal. 3:10].

Do you believe that the I AM is able to do this?

Then claim ME to be that which you want to see poured out.

Claim yourself to be that which you want to be and that you shall be.

Not because of masters will I give it unto you, but, because you have recognized ME (yourself) to be that, I will give it unto you for I AM all things to all.

Jesus would not permit Himself to be called Good Master. He knew that there is but one good and one master. He knew this one to be His Father in Heaven, the awareness of being. "The Kingdom of God" (Good) and the Kingdom of Heaven are within you [Luke 17:21].

Your belief in masters is a confession of your slavery. Only slaves have masters.

Change your conception of yourself and you will, without

the aid of masters or anyone else, automatically transform your world to conform to your changed conception of yourself.

You are told in the Book of Numbers that there was a time when men were in their own eyes as grasshoppers and because of this conception of themselves, they saw giants in the land. This is as true of man today as it was the day it was recorded. Man's conception of himself is so grasshopper-like, that he automatically makes the conditions round about him appear gigantic; in his blindness he cries out for masters to help him fight his giant problems.

Jesus tried to show man that salvation was within himself and warned him not to look for his savior in places or people.

If anyone should come saying look here or look there, believe him not, for the Kingdom of Heaven is within you [Luke 17:21].

Jesus not only refused to permit Himself to be called Good Master, He warned his followers. *"Salute no man along the highway"* [*"and greet no man along the way"* (Luke 10:4); 2 Kings 4:29*)]*. He made it clear that they should not recognize any authority or superior other than God, the Father.

Jesus established the identity of the Father as man's awareness of being. *"I and My Father are one, but My Father is greater than I"* [John 10:30; John 14:28].

I AM one with all that I am conscious of being. I AM greater than that which I am aware of being. The creator is ever greater than his creation.

"As Moses lifted up the serpent in the wilderness even so must the Son of Man be lifted up" [John 3:14]. The serpent symbolizes man's present conception of himself as a worm of the dust, living in the wilderness of human confusion. Just as Moses lifted himself from his worm-of-the-dust conception of himself to

discover God to be his awareness of being, "I AM hath sent me" [Exod. 3:14], so must you be lifted up. The day you claim, as did Moses, "I AM that I AM" [Exod. 3:14], that day your claim will blossom in the wilderness.

Your awareness is the master magician who conjures all things by being that which he would conjure. This Lord and Master that you are can and does make all that you are conscious of being appear in your world.

"No man (manifestation) cometh unto Me save My Father draw him and I and My Father are one" ["*No man can come to Me, except the Father which hath sent Me draw him: and I will raise him up at the last day*" (John 6:44); "*My Father, which gave them Me, is greater than all; and no man is able to pluck them out of My Father's hand. I and My Father are one*" (John 10:29, 30)].

You are constantly drawing to yourself that which you are conscious of being. Change your conception of yourself from that of the slave to that of Christ.

Don't be embarrassed to make this claim; only as you claim, "I AM Christ", will you do the works of Christ.

"*The works I do ye shall do also, and greater works than these shall ye do, for I go unto my Father*" ["*Truly, truly, I say to you, he who believes in Me, the works that I do, he will do also; and greater works than these he will do; because I go to the Father*" (John 14:12)]. "*He made Himself equal with God and found it not robbery to do the works of God*" [Phil. 2:6].

Jesus knew that anyone who dared to claim himself to be Christ would automatically assume the capacities to express the works of his conception of Christ.

Jesus also knew that the exclusive use of this principle of expression was not given to Him alone.

He constantly referred to His Father in Heaven.

He stated that His works would not only be equaled but that they would be surpassed by that man who dared to conceive himself to be greater than He (Jesus) had conceived Himself to be.

Jesus, in stating that He and His Father were one but that His Father was greater than He, revealed His awareness (Father) to be one with that which He was aware of being.

He found Himself as Father or awareness to be greater than that which He as Jesus was aware of being.

You and your conception of yourself are one.

You are and always will be greater than any conception you will ever have of yourself.

Man fails to do the works of Jesus Christ because he attempts to accomplish them from his present level of consciousness.

You will never transcend your present accomplishments through sacrifice and struggle.

Your present level of consciousness will only be transcended as you drop the present state and rise to a higher level.

You rise to a higher level of consciousness by taking your attention away from your present limitations and placing it upon that which you desire to be. Do not attempt this in daydreaming or wishful thinking, but in a positive manner.

Claim yourself to be the thing desired. I AM that; no sacrifice, no diet, no human tricks.

All that is asked of you is to accept your desire. If you dare claim it, you will express it.

Meditate on these: *"I rejoice not in the sacrifices of men"* [probably Mal. 1:10]. *"Not by might nor by power, but by my spirit* [Zech. 4:6]. *"Ask and you shall receive"* [Matt. 7:7; Matt. 21:22; Mark 11:24; Luke 11:9; John 15:7; John 16:24]. *"Come eat and drink without price"* [probably Isa. 55:1].

The works are finished. All that is required of you to let these qualities into expression is the claim—I AM that. Claim yourself to be that which you desire to be and that you shall be.

Expressions follow the impressions, they do not precede them. Proof that you are will follow the claim that you are, it will not precede it.

"Leave all and follow Me" [Matt. 8:22: 9:9; Luke 5:27] is a double invitation to you.

First, it invites you to turn completely away from all problems and, then, it calls upon you to continue walking in the claim that you are that which you desire to be.

Do not be a Lot's wife who looks back and becomes salted [Gen. 19] or preserved in the dead past.

Be a Lot who does not look back but who keeps his vision focused upon the promised land, the thing desired.

Do this and you will know that you have found the master, the Master Magician, making the unseen the seen through the command, "I AM THAT".

WHO AM I?

But whom say ye that I AM?

—MATTHEW 16:15

"*I AM the Lord; that is My name; and My glory will I not give to another*" [Isa. 42:8]. "*I AM the Lord, the God of all Flesh*" [Jer. 32:27].

This I AM within you, the reader, this awareness, this consciousness of being, is the Lord, the God of all Flesh.

I AM is He that should come; stop looking for another. As long as you believe in a God apart from yourself, you will continue to transfer the power of your expression to your conceptions, forgetting that you are the conceiver.

The power conceiving and the thing conceived are one but the power to conceive is greater than the conception.

Jesus discovered this glorious truth when He declared, "*I and My Father are one, but My Father is greater than I*" [John 10:30; John 14:28].

The power conceiving itself to be man is greater than its conception. All conceptions are limitations of the conceiver.

"Before Abraham was, I AM" [John 8:58]. Before the world was, I AM.

Consciousness precedes all manifestations and is the prop upon which all manifestation rests.

To remove the manifestations, all that is required of you, the conceiver, is to take your attention away from the conception. Instead of "Out of sight, out of mind", it really is "Out of mind, out of sight".

The manifestation will remain in sight only as long as it takes the force with which the conceiver—I AM—originally endowed it to spend itself. This applies to all creation from the infinitesimally small electron to the infinitely great universe.

"Be still and know that I AM God" [Ps. 46:10].

Yes, this very I AM, your awareness of being, is God, the only God. I AM is the Lord—the God of all Flesh—all manifestation.

This presence, your unconditioned awareness, comprehends neither beginning nor ending; limitations exist only in the manifestation. When you realize that this awareness is your eternal self, you will know that before Abraham was, I AM.

Begin to understand why you were told, *"Go thou and do likewise"* [Luke 10:37].

Begin now to identify yourself with this presence, your awareness, as the only reality.

All manifestations but appear to be; you as man have no reality other than that which your eternal self, I AM, believes itself to be.

"Whom do you say that I AM?" [Matt. 16:15; Mark 8:29; Luke 9:20].

This is not a question asked two thousand years ago. It is the eternal question addressed to the manifestation by the conceiver.

It is your true self, your awareness of being, asking you, its present conception of itself, "Who do you believe your awareness to be?"

This answer can be defined only within yourself, regardless of the influence of another. I AM (your true self) is not interested in man's opinion.

All its interest lies in your conviction of yourself.

What do you say of the I AM within you? Can you answer and say, "I AM Christ"?

Your answer or degree of understanding will determine the place you will occupy in life.

Do you say or believe yourself to be a man of a certain family race, nation etc.? Do you honestly believe this of yourself?

Then life, your true self will cause these conceptions to appear in your world and you will live with them as though they are real.

"I AM the door" [John 10:9]. "I AM the way" [John 14:6]. "I AM the resurrection and the life" [John 11:25]. "No man (or manifestation) cometh unto My Father save by Me" ["I am the way, the truth, and the life: no man cometh unto the Father, but by Me" (John 14:6)].

The I AM (your consciousness) is the only door through which anything can pass into your world.

Stop looking for signs. Signs follow; they do not precede. Begin to reverse the statement, "Seeing is believing", to "Believing is seeing". Start now to believe, not with the wavering confidence based on deceptive external evidence but with an undaunted confidence based on the immutable law that you can be that which you desire to be. You will find that you are not a victim of fate but a victim of faith (your own).

Only through one door can that which you seek pass into the world of manifestation. "I AM the door". Your consciousness is the door, so you must become conscious of being and having that which you desire to be and to have. Any attempt to realize your desires in ways other than through the door of consciousness makes you a thief and a robber unto yourself.

Any expression that is not felt is unnatural. Before anything appears, God, I AM, feels itself to be the thing desired; and then the thing felt appears. It is resurrected; lifted out of the nothingness.

I AM wealthy, poor, healthy, sick, free [or] confined were first of all impressions or conditions felt before they became visible expressions.

Your world is your consciousness objectified. Waste no time trying to change the outside; change the within or the impression; and the without or expression will take care of itself.

When the truth of this statement dawns upon you, you will know that you have found the lost word or the key to every door.

I AM (your consciousness) is the magical lost word which was made flesh in the likeness of that which you are conscious of being.

I AM He. Right now, I am overshadowing you, the reader, my living temple, with my presence, urging upon you a new expression. Your desires are my spoken words. My words are spirit and they are true and they shall not return unto me void but shall accomplish where unto they are sent ["*So shall my word be that goeth forth out of my mouth: it shall not return unto me void, but it shall accomplish that which I please, and it shall prosper in the thing whereto I sent it"* [Isa. 55:11)]. They are not something to be worked out.

They are garments that I, your faceless, formless self, wear. Behold! I, clothed in your desire, stand at the door (your consciousness) and knock. If you hear my voice and open unto me (recognize me as your savior), I will come in unto you and sup with you and you with me [*"Behold, I stand at the door, and knock: if any man hear my voice, and open the door, I will come in to him, and will sup with him, and he with me"* (Rev. 3:20)].

Just how my words, your desires, will be fulfilled, is not your concern. *My words have a way ye know not of* [John 4:32]. *Their ways are past finding out* [Rom. 11:33].

All that is required of you is to believe. Believe your desires to be garments your savior wears. Your belief that you are now that which you desire to be is proof of your acceptance of life's gifts. You have opened the door for your Lord, clothed in your desire, to enter the moment you establish this belief.

"When ye pray, believe that ye have received and it shall be so" [Mark 11:24]. *"All things are possible to him who believes"* [Mark 9:23].

Make the impossible possible through your belief; and the impossible (to others) will embody itself in your world.

All men have had proof of the power of faith. The faith that moves mountains is faith in yourself.

No man has faith in God who lacks confidence in himself. Your faith in God is measured by your confidence in yourself. *"I and My Father are one"* [John 10:30], man and his God are one, consciousness and manifestation are one.

And God said, *"Let there be a firmament in the midst of the waters"* [Gen. 1:6]. In the midst of all the doubts and changing opinions of others, let there be a conviction, a firmness of belief, and you shall see the dry land; your belief will appear.

The reward is to him that endureth unto the end *["But he that shall endure unto the end, the same shall be saved"* (Matt. 24:13)]. A conviction is not a conviction if it can be shaken. Your desire will be as clouds without rain unless you believe.

Your unconditioned awareness or I AM is the Virgin Mary who knew not a man [Luke 1:34] and yet, unaided by man, conceived and bore a son. Mary, the unconditioned consciousness, desired and then became conscious of being the conditioned state which she desired to express, and in a way unknown to others, became it. Go and do likewise; assume the consciousness of that which you desire to be and you, too, will give birth to your savior.

When the annunciation is made, when the urge or desire is upon you, believe it to be God's spoken word seeking embodiment through you. Go, tell no man of this holy thing that you have conceived. Lock your secret within you and magnify the Lord [Luke 1:46], magnify or believe your desire to be your savior coming to be with you.

When this belief is so firmly established that you feel confident of results, your desire will embody itself. How it will be done, no man knows. I, your desire, have ways ye know not of [John 4:32]; my ways are past finding out [Rom. 11:33]. Your desire can be likened to a seed, and seeds contain within themselves both the power and the plan of self-expression. Your consciousness is the soil. These seeds are successfully planted only if, after you have claimed yourself to be and to have that which you desire, you confidently await results without an anxious thought.

If I be lifted up in consciousness to the naturalness of my desire, I shall automatically draw the manifestation unto me.

Consciousness is the door through which life reveals itself. Consciousness is always objectifying itself.

To be conscious of being or possessing anything is to be or have that which you are conscious of being or possessing. Therefore, lift yourself to the consciousness of your desire and you will see it automatically outpicture itself.

To do this, you must deny your present identity. "Let him deny himself" [Mark 8:34]. You deny a thing by taking your attention away from it. To drop a thing, problem or ego from consciousness, you dwell upon God—God being I AM.

Be still and know that I AM is God [Ps. 46:10].

Believe, feel that I AM; know that this knowing one within you, your awareness of being, is God.

Close your eyes and feel yourself to be faceless, formless and without figure. Approach this stillness as though it were the easiest thing in the world to accomplish. This attitude will assure your success.

When all thought of problem or self is dropped from consciousness because you are now absorbed or lost in the feeling of just being I AM, then begin in this formless state to feel yourself to be that which you desire to be, "I AM that I AM".

The moment you reach a certain degree of intensity so that you actually feel yourself to be a new conception, this new feeling or consciousness is established and in due time will personify itself in the world of form.

This new perception will express itself as naturally as you now express your present identity.

To express the qualities of a consciousness naturally, you

must dwell or live within that consciousness. Appropriate it by becoming one with it. To feel a thing intensely, and then rest confidently that it is, makes the thing felt appear within your world.

"I shall stand upon my watch" [Hab. 2:1] "and see the salvation of the Lord" [2 Chron. 20:17]. I shall stand firmly upon my feeling, convinced that it is so, and see my desire appear.

"A man can receive nothing (no thing) except it be given him from Heaven" [John 3:27].

Remember, heaven is your consciousness; the Kingdom of Heaven is within you.

This is why you are warned against calling any man Father; your consciousness is the Father of all that you are.

Again you are told, "Salute no man on the highway" [Luke 10:4: 2 Kings 4:29]. See no man as an authority. Why should you ask man for permission to express when you realize that your world, in its every detail, originated within you and is sustained by you as the only conceptional center?

Your whole world may be likened to solidified space mirroring the beliefs and acceptances as projected by a formless, faceless presence, namely, I AM. Reduce the whole to its primordial substance and nothing would remain but you, a dimensionless presence, the conceiver.

The conceiver is a law apart. Conceptions under such law are not to be measured by past accomplishments or modified by present capacities for, without taking thought, the conception in a way unknown to man expresses itself.

Go within secretly and appropriate the new consciousness. Feel yourself to be it, and the former limitations shall pass away as completely and as easily as snow on a hot summer's day.

You will not even remember the former limitations; they were never part of this new consciousness.

This rebirth Jesus referred to when he said to Nicodemus, "Ye must be born again" [John 3:7], was nothing more than moving from one state of consciousness to another.

"Whatsoever ye shall ask in My name, that will I do" [John 14:13; similarly, John 15:16; John 16:23]. This certainly does not mean to ask in words, pronouncing with the lips the sounds, God or Christ Jesus, for millions have asked in this manner without results.

To feel yourself to be a thing is to have asked for that thing in His name. I AM is the nameless presence. To feel yourself to be rich is to ask for wealth in His name.

I AM is unconditioned. It is neither rich nor poor, strong nor weak. In other words, in HIM there is neither Greek nor Jew, bond nor free, male nor female. These are all conceptions or limitations of the limitless, and therefore names of the nameless.

"To feel yourself to be anything is to ask the nameless, I AM, to express that name or nature".

"Ask whatsoever ye will in My name by appropriating the nature of the thing desired and I will give it unto you".

] 6 [

I AM HE

For if ye believe not that I AM, ye shall die in your sins.

–JOHN 8:24

"All things were made by Him; and without Him was not anything made that was made" [John 1:3].

This is a hard saying for those trained in the various systems of orthodox religion to accept, but there it stands.

All things, good, bad and indifferent, were made by God. "God made man (manifestation) in His own image: in the likeness of God made He him" [Gen. 1:27]. Apparently adding to this confusion, it is stated. "And God saw that his creation was good" [Gen. 1:31].

What are you going to do about this seeming anomaly? How is man going to correlate all things as good when that which he is taught denies this fact?

Either the understanding of God is erroneous or else there is something radically wrong with man's teaching.

"To the pure all things are pure" [Titus 1:15]. This is another puzzling statement. All the good people, the pure people, the holy people, are the greatest prohibitionists. Couple the foregoing statement with this one, "There is no condemnation in Christ Jesus" *["There is therefore now no condemnation to them which are in Christ Jesus, Who walk not after the flesh, but after the Spirit"* (Rom. 8:1)*],* and you get an impassable barrier to the self-appointed judges of the world. Such statements mean nothing to the self-righteous judges blindly changing and destroying shadows. They continue in the firm belief that they are improving the world.

Man, not knowing that his world is his individual consciousness outpictured, vainly strives to conform to the opinion of others rather than to conform to the one and only opinion existent, namely, his own judgment of himself.

When Jesus discovered His consciousness to be this wonderful law of self-government, He declared, "And now I sanctify Myself that they also might be sanctified through the truth" *["And for their sakes I sanctify Myself that they also might be sanctified through the truth"* (John 17:19)*].*

He knew that consciousness was the only reality, that things objectified were nothing more than different states of consciousness.

Jesus warned His followers to seek first the Kingdom of Heaven (that state of consciousness that would produce the thing desired) and all things would be added to them [Matt. 6:33].

He also stated, *"I AM the truth"* [John 14:6]. He knew that man's consciousness was the truth or cause of all that man saw his world to be.

Jesus realized that the world was made in the likeness of man. He knew that man saw his world to be what it was because man was what he was.

In short, man's conception of himself determines that which he sees his world to be.

All things are made by God (consciousness) and without him there is nothing made that is made [John 1:3].

Creation is judged good and very good because it is the perfect likeness of that consciousness which produced it.

To be conscious of being one thing and then see yourself expressing something other than that which you are conscious of being is a violation of the law of being; therefore, it would not be good. The law of being is never broken; man ever sees himself expressing that which he is conscious of being.

Be it good, bad or indifferent, it is nevertheless a perfect likeness of his conception of himself; it is good and very good.

Not only are all things made by God, all things are made of God. All are the offspring of God. God is one. Things or divisions are the projections of the one. God being one, He must command Himself to be the seeming other for there is no other.

The absolute cannot contain something within itself that is not itself. If it did, then it would not be absolute, the only one.

Commands, to be effective, must be to oneself. "I AM that I AM" is the only effective command.

"I AM the Lord and beside Me there is none else" [Isa. 45:5; Joel 2:27].

You cannot command that which is not. As there is no other, you must command yourself to be that which you would have appear.

Let me clarify what I mean by effective command. You do not repeat like a parrot the statement, "I AM that I AM"; such vain repetition would be both stupid and fruitless.

It is not the words that make it effective; it is the consciousness of being the thing which makes it effective.

When you say, "I AM", you are declaring yourself to be. The word *that* in the statement, "I AM that I AM", indicates that which you would be. The second "I AM" in the quotation is the cry of victory.

This whole drama takes place inwardly with or without the use of words.

Be still and know that you are.

This stillness is attained by observing the observer.

Repeat quietly but with feeling, "I AM—I AM", until you have lost all consciousness of the world and know yourself just as being.

Awareness, the knowing that you are, is Almighty God: I AM.

After this is accomplished, define yourself as that which you desire to be by feeling yourself to be the thing desired: I AM *that*. This understanding that you are the thing desired will cause a thrill to course through your entire being. When the conviction is established and you really believe that you are that which you desired to be, then the second "I AM" is uttered as a cry of victory. This mystical revelation of Moses can be seen as three distinct steps: I AM; I AM free; *I really AM!*

It does not matter what the appearances round about you are like. All things make way for the coming of the Lord. I AM the Lord coming in the appearance of that which I am conscious of being. All the inhabitants of the earth cannot stay my coming or question my authority to be that which I AM conscious that I AM [*"All the inhabitants of the earth are as nothing, and He doeth according to His will in the armies of Heaven and among all the inhabitants of the earth; and none can stay His hand, nor say unto Him, 'What doest Thou?'"* (Dan. 4:35)].

"I AM the light of the world" [John 8:12], crystallizing into the form of my conception of myself.

Consciousness is the eternal light, which crystallizes only through the medium of your conception of yourself.

Change your conception of yourself and you will automatically change the world in which you live. Do not try to change people; they are only messengers telling you who you are. Revalue yourself and they will confirm the change.

Now you will realize why Jesus sanctified Himself instead of others [loan 17:19], why to the pure all things are pure [Titus 1: 15], why in Christ Jesus (the awakened consciousness) there is no condemnation [Rom. 8:1].

Awake from the sleep of condemnation and prove the principle of life. Stop not only your judgment of others but your condemnation of yourself.

Hear the revelation of the enlightened, "I know and am persuaded by the Lord Christ Jesus that there is nothing unclean of itself, but to him that seeth anything to be unclean to him it is unclean" [Rom. 14:14], and again, "Happy is the man who condemneth himself not in that which he alloweth" [*Happy is he that condemneth not himself in that thing which he alloweth*" (Rom. 14:22)].

Stop asking yourself whether or not you are worthy or unworthy to claim yourself to be that which you desire to be. You will be condemned by the world only as long as you condemn yourself.

You do not need to work out anything. The works are finished.

The principle by which all things are made and without which there is not anything made that is made is eternal.

You are this principle.

Your awareness of being is this everlasting law.

You have never expressed anything that you were not aware of being and you never will. Assume the consciousness of that which you desire to express.

Claim it until it becomes a natural manifestation. Feel it and live within that feeling until you make it your nature.

Here is a simple formula. Take your attention from your present conception of yourself and place it on that ideal of yours, the ideal you had heretofore thought beyond your reach. Claim yourself to be your ideal, not as something that you will be in time, but as that which you are in the immediate present.

Do this, and your present world of limitations will disintegrate as your new claim rises like the phoenix from its ashes.

"Be not afraid nor dismayed by reason of this great multitude; for the battle is not yours, but God's" [2 Chron. 20:15].

You do not fight against your problem; your problem will only live as long as you are conscious of it.

Take your attention away from your problem and the multitude of reasons why you cannot achieve your ideal.

Concentrate your attention entirely upon the thing desired.

"Leave all and follow me" [Matt. 8:22, 9:9; Luke 5:27].

In the face of seemingly mountainous obstacles, claim your freedom. The consciousness of freedom is the Father of freedom.

It has a way of expressing itself which no man knows.

"Ye shall not need to fight in this battle. Set yourself, stand still, and see the salvation of the Lord with you" [2 Chron. 20:17].

"I AM the Lord".

I AM (your consciousness) is the Lord. The consciousness that the thing is done, that the work is finished, is the Lord of any situation.

Listen carefully to the promise, "Ye shall not need to fight in this battle: Set yourself, stand still, and see the salvation of the Lord with you" [2 Chron. 20:17].

With you!

That particular consciousness with which you are identified is the Lord of the agreement. He will without assistance establish the thing agreed upon on earth.

Can you, in the face of the army of reasons why a thing cannot be done, quietly enter into an agreement with the Lord that it is done?

Can you, now that you have found the Lord to be your awareness of being, become aware that the battle is won?

Can you, no matter how near and threatening the enemy seems to be, continue in your confidence, standing still, knowing that the victory is yours?

If you can, you will see the salvation of the Lord.

Remember, the reward is to the one who endures [Matt. 24:13].

Stand still [Ps. 46:10].

Standing still is the deep conviction that all is well; it is done. No matter what is heard or seen, you remain unmoved, conscious of being victorious in the end.

All things are made by such agreements, and without such an agreement, there is not anything made that is made [John 1:3]. "I AM that I AM" [Exod. 3:14].

In Revelations, it is recorded that a new heaven and new earth shall appear [21:1].

John, shown this vision, was told to write, "It is done" [21:6].

Heaven is your consciousness and earth its solidified state.

Therefore, accept as did John—"It is done".

All that is required of you who seek a change is to rise to a level of that which you desire; without dwelling upon the manner of expression, record that it is done by *feeling* the naturalness of being it.

Here is an analogy that might help you to see this mystery.

Suppose you entered a motion-picture theatre just as the feature picture came to its end. All that you saw of the picture was the happy-ending. Because you wanted to see the entire story, you waited for it to unfold again. With the anti-climactic sequence, the hero is displayed as accused, surrounded by false evidence, and all that goes to wring tears from the audience. But, you, secure in the knowledge of the ending, remain calm with the understanding that, regardless of the seeming direction of the picture, the end has already been defined.

In like manner, go to the end of that which you seek; witness the happy end of it by consciously *feeling* you express and possess that which you desire to express and possess; and you, through faith, already understanding the end, will have confidence born of this knowledge.

This knowledge will sustain you through the necessary interval of time that it takes the picture to unfold.

Ask no help of man; *feel*, "It is done", by consciously claiming yourself to be, now, that which as man you hope to be.

] **7** [

THY WILL BE DONE

Not My will, but Thine, be done.

—Luke 22:42

"Not My will, but Thine, be done" *[*(Luke 22:42); *"O My Father, if this cup may not pass away from Me, except I drink it, Thy will be done"* (Matt. 26:42); *"Nevertheless not what I will, but what Thou wilt"* (Mark 14:36)*]*. This resignation is not one of blind realization that "I can of Myself do nothing, the Father within Me, He doeth the work" *["I can of Mine own Self do nothing: as I hear, I judge: and My judgment is just; because I seek not Mine own will, but the will of the Father which hath sent Me"* (John 5:30); *"Believest thou not that I am in the Father, and the Father in Me? the words that I speak unto you I speak not of Myself: but the Father that dwelleth in Me, He doeth the works"* (John 14:10)*]*.

When man wills, he attempts to make something which does not now exist appear in time and space.

Too often we are not aware of that which we are really doing.

We unconsciously state that we do not possess the capacities to express.

We predicate our desire upon the hope of acquiring the necessary capacities in future time. "I AM not, but I will be".

Man does not realize that consciousness is the Father which does the work, so he attempts to express that which he is not conscious of being.

Such struggles are doomed to failure; only the present expresses itself.

Unless I am conscious of being that which I seek, I will not find it.

God (your awareness) is the substance and fullness of all.

God's will is the recognition of that which is, not of that which will be.

Instead of seeing this saying as "Thine will be done", see it as "Thy will is done".

The works are finished.

The principle by which all things are made visible is eternal.

"Eyes have not seen nor ears heard, neither hath it entered into the hearts of men, the things which God hath prepared for those who love the law" *["Eye hath not seen nor ear heard, neither hath entered into the heart of man, the things which God hath prepared for them that love Him"* (1 Cor. 2:9–10)].

When a sculptor looks at a formless piece of marble he sees, buried within its formless mass, his finished piece of art. The sculptor, instead of making his masterpiece, merely reveals it by removing that part of the marble which hides his conception.

The same applies to you. In your formless awareness lies buried all that you will ever conceive yourself to be.

The recognition of this truth will transform you from an

unskilled laborer who tries to make it so to a great artist who recognizes it to be so.

Your claim that you are now that which you want to be will remove the veil of human darkness and reveal your claim perfectly; I AM that.

God's will was expressed in the words of the Widow, "It is well".

Man's will would have been, "It will be well". To state, "I shall be well", is to say, "I am ill".

God, the Eternal Now, is not mocked by words or vain repetition.

God continually personifies that which is.

Thus, the resignation of Jesus (who made Himself equal with God) was turning from the recognition of lack (which the future indicates with "I shall be") to the recognition of supply by claiming, "I AM that; it is done; thank You, Father".

Now you will see the wisdom in the words of the prophet when he states. "Let the weak say, I AM strong" [Joel 3:10].

Man in his blindness will not heed the prophet's advice: he continues to claim himself to be weak, poor, wretched and all the other undesirable expressions from which he is trying to free himself by ignorantly claiming that he will be free from these characteristics in the expectancy of the future.

Such thoughts thwart the one law that can ever free him.

There is only one door through which that which you seek can enter your world. "I AM the door" [John 10:9].

When you say, "I AM", you are declaring yourself to be, first person, present tense; there is no future.

To know that I AM is to be conscious of being. Consciousness is the only door.

Unless you are conscious of being that which you seek, you seek in vain.

If you judge after appearances, you will continue to be enslaved by the evidence of your senses.

To break this hypnotic spell of the senses, you are told, "Go within and shut the door" *["But thou, when thou prayest, enter into thy closet, and when thou hast shut thy door, pray to thy Father which is in secret; and thy Father which seeth in secret shall reward thee openly" (Matt. 6:6); "Enter thou into thy chambers, and shut thy doors about thee: hide thyself as it were for a little moment, until the indignation be overpast" (Isa. 26:20); "And when thou art come in, thou shalt shut the door upon thee and upon thy sons" (2 Kings 4:4); "He went in therefore, and shut the door upon them twain, and prayed unto the Lord" (2 Kings 4:33)].*

The door of the senses must be tightly shut before your new claim can be honored.

Closing the door of the senses is not as difficult as it appears to be at first.

It is done without effort.

It is impossible to serve two masters at the same time [Matt. 6:24; Luke 16:13].

The master man serves is that which he is conscious of being. I am Lord and Master of that which I am conscious of being.

It is no effort for me to conjure poverty if I am conscious of being poor.

My servant (poverty) is compelled to follow me (conscious of poverty) as long as I AM (the Lord) conscious of being poor.

Instead of fighting against the evidence of the senses, you claim yourself to be that which you desire to be.

As your attention is placed on this claim, the doors of the senses automatically close against your former master (that which you were conscious of being).

As you become lost in the feeling of being (that which you are now claiming to be true of yourself), the doors of the senses once more open, revealing your world to be the perfect expression of that which you are conscious of being.

Let us follow the example of Jesus who realized, as man, He could do nothing to change His present picture of lack.

He closed the door of His senses against His problem and went to His Father, the one to Whom all things are possible [Matt. 19:26; Mark 9:23, 10:27, 14:36; Luke 18:27; Acts 8:37].

Having denied the evidence of His senses, He claimed Himself to be all that, a moment before, His senses told him He was not.

Knowing that consciousness expresses its likeness on earth, He remained in the claimed consciousness until the doors (His senses) opened and confirmed the rulership of the Lord.

Remember. I AM is Lord of all. Never again use the will of man which claims, "I will be".

Be as resigned as Jesus and claim, "I AM that".

] 8 [

NO OTHER GOD

I am the first, and I am the last: and beside Me is no God.

—Isaiah 44:6

I am the Lord thy God, which brought thee out of the land of
Egypt, from the house of bondage.

Thou shalt have none other gods before Me.

—Deuteronomy 5:6, 7

"Thou shalt have no other God beside Me". As long as
man entertains a belief in a power apart from himself,
so long will he rob himself of the being that he is.

Every belief in powers apart from himself, whether for
good or evil, will become the mould of the graven image worshipped.

The beliefs in the potency of drugs to heal, diets to
strengthen, moneys to secure, are the values or money changers that must be thrown out of the power [Matt. 21:12; Mark
11:15; Luke 19:45; John 2:14,15] he can then unfailingly manifest that quality.

This understanding throws out the money changers Temple. "Ye are the Temple of the Living God" *[*(1 Cor. 3:16, 6:19); *"And what agreement hath the temple of God with idols? for ye are the temple of the living God; as God hath said, I will dwell in them, and walk in them; and I will be their God, and they shall be my people"* (2 Cor. 6:16)*]*, a Temple made without hands.

It is written, "My house shall be called of all nations a house of prayer, but ye have made it a den of thieves" *[*(Matt. 21:13); *". . . for Mine house shall be called an house of prayer for all people"* (Isa. 56:7)*]*.

The thieves who rob you are your own false beliefs. It is your belief in a thing not the thing itself that aids you. There is only one power: I AM He. Because of your belief in external things, you think power into them by transferring the power that you are to the external thing. Realize you yourself are the power you have mistakenly given to outer conditions.

The Bible compares the opinionated man to the camel who could not go through the needle's eye [Matt. 19:24; Mark 10:25; Luke 18:25]. The needle's eye referred to was a small gate in the walls of Jerusalem, which was so narrow that a camel could not go through it until relieved of its pack.

The rich man, that is the one burdened with false human concepts, cannot enter the Kingdom of Heaven until relieved of his burden [Matt. 19:23] any more than could the camel go through this small gate.

Man feels so secure in his man-made laws, opinions and beliefs that he invests them with an authority they do not possess.

Satisfied that his knowledge is all, he remains unaware that all outward appearances are but states of mind externalized.

When he realizes that the consciousness of a quality externalizes that quality without the aid of any other or many values and establishes the one true value, his own consciousness.

"The Lord is in His holy temple" [Hab. 2:20]. Consciousness dwells within that which it is conscious of being. I AM is the Lord and man, his temple.

Knowing that consciousness objectifies itself, man must forgive all men for being that which they are.

He must realize that all are expressing (without the aid of another) that which they are conscious of being.

Peter, the enlightened or disciplined man, knew that a change of consciousness would produce a change of expression.

Instead of sympathizing with the beggars of life at the temple's gate, he declared, "Silver and gold have I none (for thee), but such as I have (the consciousness of freedom), give I unto thee" [Acts 3:6].

"Stir up the gift within you" *["Wherefore I put thee in remembrance that thou stir up the gift of God, which is in thee"* (2 Tim. 1:6)*].*

Stop begging and claim yourself to be that which you decide to be. Do this and you too will jump from your crippled world into the world of freedom, singing praises to the Lord, I AM.

"Far greater is He that is in you than he that is in the world" *["Ye are of God, little children, and have overcome them: because greater is He that is in you, than he that is in the world"* (1 John 4:4)*].*

This is the cry of everyone who finds his awareness of being to be God.

Your recognition of this fact will automatically cleanse the temple, your consciousness, of the thieves and robbers, restoring to you that dominion over things, which you lost the moment you forgot the command, "Thou shalt have no other God beside ME".

THE FOUNDATION STONE

Let every man take heed how he buildeth thereon. For other foundations can no man lay than that is laid, which is Jesus Christ. Now if man build upon this foundation gold, silver, precious stones, wood, hay, stubble; every man's work shall be made manifest; for the day shall declare it.

–1 Corinthians 3:10–13

The foundation of all expression is consciousness.

Try as man will, he cannot find a cause of manifestation other than his consciousness of being.

Man thinks he has found the cause of disease in germs, the cause of war in conflicting political ideologies and greed. All such discoveries of man, catalogued as the essence of Wisdom, are foolishness in the eyes of God.

There is only one power and this power is God (consciousness).

It kills; it makes alive; it wounds: it heals: it does all things, good, bad or indifferent. Man moves in a world that is nothing more or less than his consciousness objectified.

Not knowing this, he wars against his reflections while he keeps alive the light and the images which project the reflections.

"I AM the light of the world" [John 8:12]. I AM (consciousness) is the light.

That which I am conscious of being (my conception of myself)—such as "I am rich", "I am healthy", "I am free"—are the images.

The world is the mirror magnifying all that I AM conscious of being.

Stop trying to change the world since it is only the mirror. Man's attempt to change the world by force is as fruitless as breaking a mirror in the hope of changing his face. Leave the mirror and change your face. Leave the world alone and change your conceptions of yourself. The reflection then will be satisfactory.

Freedom or imprisonment, satisfaction or frustration can only be differentiated by the consciousness of being.

Regardless of your problem, its duration or its magnitude, careful attention to these instructions will in an amazingly short time eliminate even the memory of the problem.

Ask yourself this question: "How would I feel if I were free?" The very moment you sincerely ask this question, the answer comes.

No man can tell another the satisfaction of his desire fulfilled.

It remains for each within himself to experience the feeling and joy of this automatic change of consciousness.

The feeling or thrill that comes to one in response to his

self-questioning is the Father state of consciousness or Foundation Stone upon which the conscious change is built.

Just how this feeling will embody itself no one knows, but it will; the Father (consciousness) has ways that no man knows [Rom. 11:33]; it is the unalterable law.

All things express their nature. As you wear a feeling, it becomes your nature.

It might take a moment or a year—it is entirely dependent upon the degree of conviction. As doubts vanish and you can feel "I AM this", you begin to develop the fruit or the nature of the thing you are feeling yourself to be.

When a person buys a new hat or pair of shoes, he thinks everyone knows that they are new. He feels unnatural with his newly acquired apparel until it becomes a part of him. The same applies to the wearing of the new states of consciousness.

When you ask yourself the question, "How would I feel if my desire were at this moment realized?" the automatic reply, until it is properly conditioned by time and use, is actually disturbing.

The period of adjustment to realize this potential of consciousness is comparable to the newness of the wearing apparel.

Not knowing that consciousness is ever outpicturing itself in conditions round about you, like Lot's wife, you continually look back upon your problem and again become hypnotized by its seeming naturalness [Gen. 19].

Heed the words of Jesus (salvation): "Leave all and follow Me" [Matt. 4:19; Matt. 8:22; Matthew 16:24; Matthew 19:21; Mark 1:17; Mark 8:34; Mark 10:21; Luke 9:23; Luke 18:22]. "*Let* the dead bury the dead" [Matt. 8:22; Luke 9:60].

Your problem might have you so hypnotized by its seeming reality and naturalness that you find it difficult to wear the new feeling or consciousness of your savior.

You must assume this garment if you would have results.

The stone (consciousness) which the builders rejected (would not wear) is the chief cornerstone, and other foundations no man can lay.

] 10 [

TO HIM THAT HATH

Take heed therefore how ye hear; for whosoever hath, to him shall be given; and whosoever hath not, from him shall be taken even that which he seemeth to have.

—LUKE 8:18

The Bible, which is the greatest psychological book ever written, warns man to be aware of what he hears; then follows this warning with the statement. "To him that hath it shall be given and to him that hath not it shall be taken away".

Though many look upon this statement as one of the most cruel and unjust of the sayings attributed to Jesus, it still remains a just and merciful law based upon life's changeless principle of expression.

Man's ignorance of the working of the law does not excuse him nor save him from the results.

Law is impersonal and therefore no respecter of persons [Acts 10:34; Rom. 2:11]. Man is warned to be selective in that which he hears and accepts as true.

Everything that man accepts as true leaves an impression

on his consciousness and must in time be defined as proof or disproof.

Perceptive hearing is the perfect medium through which man registers impressions.

A man must discipline himself to hear only that which he wants to hear, regardless of rumors or the evidence of his senses to the contrary.

As he conditions his perceptive hearing, he will react only to those impressions which he has decided upon.

This law never fails.

Fully conditioned, man becomes incapable of hearing other than that which contributes to his desire.

God, as you have discovered, is that unconditioned awareness which gives to you all that you are aware of being.

To be aware of being or having anything is to be or have that which you are aware of being.

Upon this changeless principle all things rest.

It is impossible for anything to be other than that which it is aware of being.

"To him that hath (that which he is aware of being) it shall be given". Good, bad or indifferent—it does not matter—man receives multiplied a hundredfold that which he is aware of being. In keeping with this changeless law, "To him that hath not, it shall be taken from him and added to the one that hath", the rich get richer and the poor get poorer. You can only magnify that which you are conscious of being.

All things gravitate to that consciousness with which they are in tune.

Likewise, all things disentangle themselves from that consciousness with which they are out of tune.

Divide the wealth of the world equally among all men and

in a short time, this equal division will be as originally dispro-portioned. Wealth will find its way back into the pockets of those from whom it was taken.

Instead of joining the chorus of the have-nots who insist on destroying those who have, recognize this changeless law of expression. Consciously define yourself as that which you desire.

Once defined, your conscious claim established, continue in this confidence until the reward is received.

As surely as the day follows the night, any attribute, con-sciously claimed, will manifest itself.

Thus, that which to the sleeping orthodox world is a cruel and unjust law becomes to the enlightened one of the most merciful and just statements of truth.

"I am come not to destroy but to fulfill" [Matt. 5:17]. Nothing is actually destroyed. Any seeming destruction is a result of a change in consciousness.

Consciousness ever fills full the state in which it dwells.

The state from which consciousness is detached seems to those not familiar with this law to be destructive.

However, this is only preparatory to a new state of con-sciousness.

Claim yourself to be that which you want filled full.

"Nothing is destroyed. All is fulfilled".

"To him that hath it shall be given".

] **11** [

CHRISTMAS

Behold, a virgin shall be with child and shall bring forth a Son, and they shall call His name Emmanuel, which being interpreted is God with us.

—MATTHEW 1:23

One of the most controversial statements in the New Testament concerns the virgin conception and subsequent birth of Jesus, a conception in which man had no part. It is recorded that a Virgin conceived a Son without the aid of man, then secretly and without effort gave birth to her conception.

This is the foundation upon which all Christendom rests.

The Christian world is asked to believe this story, for man must believe the unbelievable to fully express the greatness that he is.

Scientifically, man might be inclined to discard the whole Bible as untrue because his reason will not permit him to believe that the virgin birth is physiologically possible, but the Bible is a message of the soul and must be interpreted psychologically if man is to discover its true symbology.

Man must see this story as a psychological drama rather than a statement of physical fact. In so doing, he will discover the Bible to be based on a law which, if self-applied, will result in a manifested expression transcending his wildest dreams of accomplishment. To apply this law of self-expression, man must be schooled in the belief and disciplined to stand upon the platform that "all things are possible to God" [Matt. 19:26; Mark 9:23, 10:27, 14:36; Luke 18:27; Acts 8:37].

The outstanding dramatic dates of the New Testament, namely, the birth, death and resurrection of Jesus, were timed and dated to coincide with certain astronomical phenomena.

The mystics who recorded this story noticed that at certain seasons of the year beneficial changes on earth coincided with astronomical changes above.

In writing this psychological drama, they have personified the story of the soul as the biography of man.

Using these cosmic changes, they have marked the Birth and Resurrection of Jesus to convey that the same beneficial changes take place psychologically in the consciousness of man as he follows the law.

Even to those who fail to understand it, the story of Christmas is one of the most beautiful stories ever told.

When unfolded in the light of its mystic symbology, it is revealed as the true birth of every manifestation in the world.

This virgin birth is recorded as having taken place on December 25th or, as certain secret societies celebrate it, on Christmas Eve, at midnight of December 24th.

Mystics established this date to mark the birth of Jesus because it was in keeping with the great earthly benefits this astronomical change signifies.

The astronomical observations which prompted the authors

of this drama to use these dates were all made in the northern hemisphere; so from an astronomical point of view, the reverse would be true if seen from the southern latitudes.

However, this story was recorded in the north and therefore was based on northern observation.

Man very early discovered that the sun played a most important part in his life, that without the sun, physical life as he knew it could not be.

So these most important dates in the story of the life of Jesus are based upon the position of the sun as seen from the earth in the northern latitudes.

After the sun reaches its highest point in the heavens in June, it gradually falls southward, taking with it the life of the plant world so that by December almost all of nature has been stilled.

Should the sun continue to fall southward, all nature would be stilled unto death.

However, on December 25th, the sun begins its great move northward, bringing with it the promise of salvation and life anew for the world. Each day, as the sun rises higher in the heavens, man gains confidence in being saved from death by cold and starvation, for he knows that as it moves northward and crosses the equator all nature will rise again, will be resurrected from its long winter sleep.

Our day is measured from midnight to midnight, and, since the visible day begins in the east and ends in the west, the ancients said the day was born of that constellation which occupied the eastern horizon at midnight. On Christmas Eve, or midnight of December 24th, the constellation Virgo is rising on the eastern horizon.

So it is recorded that this Son and Savior of the world was born of a virgin.

It is also recorded that this virgin mother was traveling through the night, that she stopped at an inn and was given the only available room among the animals and there in a manger, where the animals fed, the shepherds found the Holy Child.

The animals with whom the Holy Virgin was lodged are the holy animals of the zodiac. There in that constantly moving circle of astronomical animals stands the Holy Mother. Virgo, and there you will see her every midnight of December 24th, standing on the eastern horizon as the sun and savior of the world starts his journey northward.

Psychologically, this birth takes place in man on that day when man discovers his consciousness to be the sun and savior of his world. When man knows the significance of this mystical statement, "I am the light of the world" [Matt. 5:14; John 8:12], he will realize that his I AM, or consciousness, is the sun of his life, which sun radiates images upon the screen of space. These images are in the likeness of that which he, as man, is conscious of being. Thus qualities and attributes which appear to move upon the screen of his world are really projections of this light from within himself.

The numberless unrealized hopes and ambitions of man are the seeds which are buried within the consciousness or virgin womb of man. There they remain like the seeds of earth, held in the frozen waste of winter, waiting for the sun to move northward or for man to return to the knowledge of who he is. In returning he moves northward through recognition of his true self by claiming "I AM the light of the world".

When man discovers his consciousness or I AM to be God, the savior of his world, he will be as the sun in its northern passage.

All hidden urges and ambitions will then be warmed and stimulated into birth by this knowledge of his true self.

He will claim that he is that which heretofore he hoped to be.

Without the aid of any man, he will define himself as that which he desires to express.

He will discover that his I AM is the virgin conceiving without the aid of man, that all conceptions of himself, when felt, and fixed in consciousness, will be embodied easily as living realities in his world.

Man will one day realize that this whole drama takes place in his consciousness, that his unconditioned consciousness or I AM is the Virgin Mary desiring to express, that through this law of self-expression he defines himself as that which he desires to express and that without the help or cooperation of anyone he will express that which he has consciously claimed and defined himself as being.

He will then understand: why Christmas is fixed on December 25th, while Easter is a movable date; why upon the virgin conception the whole of Christendom rests; that his consciousness is the virgin womb or bride of the Lord receiving impressions as self-impregnations and then without assistance embodying these impressions as the expressions of his life.

] 12 [

CRUCIFIXION AND RESURRECTION

I AM the Resurrection and the Life; he that believeth in Me, though he were dead, yet shall he live.

—JOHN 11:25

The mystery of the crucifixion and the resurrection is so interwoven that, to be fully understood, the two must be explained together for one determines the other. This mystery is symbolized on earth in the rituals of Good Friday and Easter. You have observed that the anniversary of this cosmic event, announced every year by the church, is not a fixed date as are other anniversaries marking births and deaths, but that this day changes from year to year, falling anywhere from the 22nd day of March to the 25th day of April.

The day of resurrection is determined in this manner. The first Sunday after the full moon in Aries is celebrated as Easter. Aries begins on the 21st day of March and ends approximately on the 19th day of April. The sun's entry into Aries marks the beginning of Spring. The moon in its monthly transit around the earth will form sometime between March 21st and April

25th an opposition to the sun, which opposition is called a full moon. The first Sunday after this phenomenon of the heavens occurs is celebrated as Easter; the Friday preceding this day is observed as Good Friday.

This movable date should tell the observant one to look for some interpretation other than the one commonly accepted. These days do not mark the anniversaries of the death and resurrection of an individual who lived on earth.

Seen from the earth, the sun in its northern passage appears at the Spring season of the year to cross the imaginary line man calls the equator. So it is said by the mystic to be crossified or crucified that man might live. It is significant that soon after this event takes place, all nature begins to arise or resurrect itself from its long Winter's sleep. Therefore, it may be concluded that this disturbance of nature, at this season of the year, is due directly to this crossing. Thus, it is believed that the sun must shed its blood on the Passover.

If these days marked the death and resurrection of a man, they would be fixed so that they would fall on the same date every year as all other historical events are fixed, but obviously this is not the case.

These dates were not intended to mark the anniversaries of the death and resurrection of Jesus, the man.

The scriptures are psychological dramas and will reveal their meaning only as they are interpreted psychologically.

These dates are adjusted to coincide with the cosmic change which occurs at this time of the year, marking the death of the old year and the beginning or resurrecting of the new year or Spring. These dates do symbolize the death and resurrection of the Lord; but this Lord is not a man; it is your awareness of being.

It is recorded that He gave His life that you might live, "I AM come that you might have life and that you might have it more abundantly" [John 10:10]. Consciousness slays itself by detaching itself from that which it is conscious of being so that it may live to that which it desires to be.

Spring is the time of year when the millions of seeds, which all Winter lay buried in the ground, suddenly spring into visibility that man might live; and, because the mystical drama of the crucifixion and resurrection is in the nature of this yearly change, it is celebrated at this Spring season of the year; but, actually, it is taking place every moment of time.

The being who is crucified is your awareness of being. The cross is your conception of yourself. The resurrection is the lifting into visibility of this conception of yourself.

Far from being a day of mourning, Good Friday should be a day of rejoicing, for there can be no resurrection or expression unless there is first a crucifixion or impression.

The thing to be resurrected in your case is that which you desire to be.

To do this, you must feel yourself to be the thing desired.

You must feel "I AM the resurrection and the life of the desire".

I AM (your awareness of being) is the power resurrecting and making alive that which in your awareness you desire to be.

"Two shall agree on touching anything and I shall establish it on earth" *["Again I say unto you, That if two of you shall agree on earth as touching any thing that they shall ask, it shall be done for them of my Father which is in heaven (Matt. 18:19)].*

The two agreeing are you (your awareness—the consciousness desiring) and the thing desired. When this agreement is attained, the crucifixion is completed; two have crossed or crossified each other.

I AM and THAT—consciousness and that which you are conscious of being—have joined and are one; I AM now nailed or fixed in the belief that I AM this fusion.

Jesus or I AM is nailed upon the cross of *that*.

The nail that binds you upon the cross is the nail of feeling.

The mystical union is now consummated and the result will be the birth of a child or the resurrection of a son bearing witness of his Father.

Consciousness is united to that which it is conscious of being.

The world of expression is the child confirming this union.

The day you cease to be conscious of being that which you are now conscious of being, that day your child or expression shall die and return to the bosom of his father, the faceless, formless awareness.

All expressions are the results of such mystical unions.

So the priests are correct when they say that true marriages are made in heaven and can only be dissolved in heaven.

But let me clarify this statement by telling you that heaven is not a locality; it is a state of consciousness.

The Kingdom of Heaven is within you [Luke 17:21].

In heaven (consciousness) God is touched by that which he is aware of being. "Who has touched me? For I perceive virtue has gone out of me" [*"Who touched me? And Jesus said. Somebody hath touched me: for I perceive that virtue is gone out of me"* (Luke 8:45, 46; Mark 5:30)].

The moment this touching (feeling) takes place, there is an offspring or going-out-of-me into visibility taking place.

The day man feels "I AM free", "I AM wealthy", "I AM

strong", God (I AM) is touched or crucified by these qualities or virtues.

The results of such touching or crucifying will be seen in the birth or resurrection of the qualities felt, for man must have visible confirmation of all that he is conscious of being.

Now you will know why man or manifestation is always made in the image of God.

Your awareness imag[in]es and outpictures all that you are aware of being.

"I AM the Lord and besides me there is no God" [Isa. 45:5,6]. "I AM the Resurrection and the Life" [John 11:25].

You shall become fixed in the belief that you are that which you desire to be. Before you have any visible proof that you are, you will, from the deep conviction which you have felt fixed within you, know that you are; and so, without waiting for the confirmation of your senses, you will cry, "It is finished" [John 19:30].

Then, with a faith born of the knowledge of this changeless law, you will be as one dead and entombed; you will be still and unmoved in your conviction and confident that you will resurrect the qualities that you have fixed and are feeling within you.

] 13 [

THE I'M-PRESSIONS

And as we have borne the image of the earthly, we shall also bear
the image of the heavenly.

—1 Corinthians 15:49

Your consciousness or your I AM is the unlimited potential upon which impressions are made.

I'm-pressions are defined states pressed upon your I AM.

Your consciousness or your I AM can be likened to a sensitive film. In the virgin state, it is potentially unlimited.

You can impress or record a message of love or a hymn of
hate, a wonderful symphony or discordant jazz. It does not
matter what the nature of the impression might be; your I
AM will, without a murmur, willingly receive and sustain all
impressions.

Your consciousness is the one referred to in Isaiah 53:3–7.

*"He is despised and rejected of men; a man of sorrows, and ac-
quainted with grief: and we hid as it were our faces from Him, He
was despised, and we esteemed Him not".*

"Surely He hath borne our grieves, and carried our sorrows: yet we did esteem Him stricken, smitten of God, and afflicted".

"But He was wounded for our transgressions, He was bruised for our iniquities: the chastisement of our peace was upon him; and with his stripes we are healed".

"All we like sheep have gone astray; we have turned every one to his own way; and the Lord hath laid on Him the iniquity of us all".

"He was oppressed, and He was afflicted,
yet He opened not his mouth:
He is brought as a lamb to the slaughter
and as a sheep before her shearers is dumb,
so He openeth not His mouth."

Your unconditioned consciousness is impersonal; it is no respecter of persons [Acts 10:34; Rom. 2:11].

Without thought or effort, it automatically expresses every impression that is registered upon it. It does not object to any impression that is placed upon it for; although it is capable of receiving and expressing any and all defined states, it remains forever an immaculate and an unlimited potential.

Your I AM is the foundation upon which the defined state or conception of yourself rests; but it is not defined by, nor is it dependent on, such defined states for its being.

Your I AM neither expands nor contracts; nothing alters or adds to it. Before any defined state was, IT is. When all states cease to be, IT is. All defined states or conceptions of yourself are but ephemeral expressions of your eternal being.

To be impressed is to be I'm-pressed (I AM pressed—first person—present tense). All expressions are the result of

I'm-pressions. Only as you claim yourself to be that which you desire to be will you express such desires.

Let all desires become impressions of qualities that are, not of qualities that will be. I'm (your awareness) is God and God is the fullness of all, the Eternal NOW, I AM.

Take no thought of tomorrow; tomorrow's expressions are determined by today's impressions.

"Now is the accepted time" [2 Cor. 6:2; Isa. 49:8]. "The Kingdom of Heaven is at hand" [Matt. 4:17]. Jesus (salvation) said, "I am with you always" [Matt. 28:20]. Your awareness is the savior that is with you always; but, if you deny Him, He will deny you also [Matt. 10:33; Luke 12:9]. You deny Him by claiming that He will appear, as millions today are claiming that salvation is to come; this is the equivalent of saying, "We are not saved".

You must stop looking for your savior to appear and begin claiming that you are already saved, and the signs of your claims will follow.

When the widow was asked what she had in her house, there was recognition of substance; her claim was a few drops of oil [4 Kings 4:1–6]. A few drops will become a gusher if properly claimed.

Your awareness magnifies all consciousness.

To claim that I shall have oil (joy) is to confess that I have empty measures.

Such impressions of lack produce lack.

God, your awareness, is no respecter of persons [Acts 10:34; Rom. 2:11]. Purely impersonal, God, this awareness of all existence, receives impressions, qualities and attributes defining consciousness, namely, your impressions.

Your every desire should be determined by need. Needs, whether seeming or real, will automatically be fulfilled when they are welcomed with sufficient intensity of purpose as defined desires.

Knowing that your awareness is God, you should look upon each desire as the spoken word of God, telling you that which is.

"Cease ye from man, whose breath is in his nostrils: for wherein is he to be accounted of?" [Isa. 2:22].

We are ever that which is defined by our awareness. Never claim, "I shall be that". Let all claims from now on be, "I AM that I AM". Before we ask, we are answered. The solution of any problem associated with desire is obvious. Every problem automatically produces the desire of solution.

Man is schooled in the belief that his desires are things against which he must struggle. In his ignorance, he denies his savior who is constantly knocking at the door of consciousness to be let in *(I AM the door)*.

Would not your desire, if realized, save you from your problem?

To let your savior in is the easiest thing in the world.

Things must be, to be let in.

You are conscious of a desire; the desire is something you are aware of now.

Your desire, though invisible, must be affirmed by you to be something that is real. "God calleth those things which be not (are not seen) as though they were" [Rom. 4:17]. Claiming I AM the thing desired. I let the savior in.

"Behold, I stand at the door, and knock: if any man hear My voice, and open the door, I will come in to him, and will sup with him, and he with Me" [Rev. 3:20].

Every desire is the savior's knock at the door.

This knock every man hears.

Man opens the door when he claims, "I AM He". See to it that you let your savior in.

Let the thing desired press itself upon you until you are I'm-pressed with nowness of your savior; then you utter the cry of victory, *"It is finished"* [John 19:30].

CIRCUMCISION

In whom also ye are circumcised with the circumcision made without hands; in putting off the body of the sins of the flesh by circumcision of Christ.

—COLOSSIANS 2:11

Circumcision is the operation which removes the veil that hides the head of creation.

The physical act has nothing to do with the spiritual act.

The whole world could be physically circumcised and yet remain unclean and blind leaders of the blind.

The spiritually circumcised have had the veil of darkness removed and know themselves to be Christ, the light of the world.

Let me now perform the spiritual operation on you, the reader.

This act is performed on the eighth day after birth, not because this day has any special significance or in any way differs from other days, but it is performed on this eighth day because eight is the figure which has neither beginning nor end.

Furthermore, the ancients symbolized the eighth numeral or letter as an enclosure or veil within and behind which lay buried the mystery of creation.

Thus, the secret of the operation on the eighth day is in keeping with the nature of the act, which act is to reveal the eternal head of creation, that changeless something in which all things begin and end and yet which remains its eternal self when all things cease to be.

This mysterious something is your awareness of being.

At this moment you are aware of being, but you are also aware of being someone.

This someone is the veil that hides the being you really are.

You are first conscious of being, then you are conscious of being man. After the veil of man is placed upon your faceless self, you become conscious of being a member of a certain race, nation, family, creed etc.

The veil to be lifted in spiritual circumcision is the veil of man.

But before this can be done, you must cut away the adhesions of race, nation, family and so on.

"In Christ there is neither Greek nor Jew, bond nor free, male nor female" ["... a renewal in which there is no distinction between Greek and Jew, circumcised and uncircumcised, barbarian, Scythian, slave and freeman, but Christ is all, and in all" (Col. 3:11)].

"You must leave father, mother, brother and follow me" ["If anyone comes to Me, and does not hate his own father and mother and wife and children and brothers and sisters, yes, and even his own life, he cannot be My disciple" (Luke 14:26)].

To accomplish this you stop identifying yourself with these

divisions by becoming indifferent to such claims. Indifference is the knife that severs. *Feeling* is the tie that binds.

When you can look upon man as one grand brotherhood without distinction of race or creed, then you will know that you have severed these adhesions.

With these ties cut, all that now separates you from your true being is your belief that you are man.

To remove this last veil, you drop your conception of yourself as man by knowing yourself just to be.

Instead of the consciousness of "I AM man", let there be just "I AM"—faceless, formless and without figure.

You are spiritually circumcised when the consciousness of man is dropped and your unconditioned awareness of being is revealed to you as the everlasting head of creation, a formless, faceless all-knowing presence.

Then, unveiled and awake, you will declare and know that—I AM is God and beside me, this awareness, there is no God.

This mystery is told symbolically in the Bible story of Jesus washing the feet of his disciples. It is recorded that Jesus laid aside his garments and took a towel and girded himself. Then, after washing his disciples' feet, he wiped them with the towel wherewith he was girded. Peter protested the washing of his feet and was told that unless his feet were washed he would have no part of Jesus. Peter on hearing this replied, "Lord, not my feet only, but also my hands and my head". Jesus answered and said, "He that is washed needeth not save to wash his feet, but is clean every whit" [John 13:1–10].

Common sense would tell the reader that a man is not clean all over just, because his feet are washed. Therefore, he should either discard this story as fantastic or else look for its hidden meaning.

Every story of the Bible is a psychological drama taking place in the consciousness of man, and this one is no exception. This washing of the disciples' feet is the mystical story of spiritual circumcision or the revealing of the secrets of the Lord.

Jesus is called the Lord. You are told that the Lord's name is I AM—Je Suis. "I AM the Lord that is my name", Isaiah 42:8. The story states that Jesus was naked save for a towel which covered his loins or secrets. Jesus or Lord symbolizes your awareness of being whose secrets are hidden by the towel (consciousness of man). The foot symbolizes the understanding which must be washed of all human beliefs or conceptions of itself by the Lord.

As the towel is removed to dry the feet, the secrets of the Lord are revealed.

In short, the removing of the belief that you are man reveals your awareness as the head of creation. Man is the foreskin hiding the head of creation. I AM the Lord hidden by the veil of man.

] 15 [

INTERVAL OF TIME

Let not your heart be troubled; ye believe in God, believe also in
Me. In My Father's house are many mansions; if it were not so, I
would have told you. I go to prepare a place for you. And if I go
and prepare a place for you, I will come again, and receive you
unto Myself; that where I am, there ye may be also.

—JOHN 14:1–3

"Let not your heart be troubled; ye believe in God, believe also in me. In my Father's house are many mansions; if it were not so, I would have told you. I go to prepare
a place for you. And if I go and prepare a place for you, I will
come again, and receive you unto myself; that where I am,
there ye may be also".

The ME in whom you must believe is your consciousness,
the I AM; it is God.

It is also the Father's house containing within itself all conceivable states of consciousness.

Every conditioned state of consciousness is called a mansion. This conversation takes place within yourself.

Your I AM, the unconditioned consciousness, is the Christ Jesus speaking to the conditioned self or the John Smith consciousness.

"I AM John", from a mystical point of view, is two beings, namely, Christ and John.

So I go to prepare a place for you, moving from your present state of consciousness into that state desired.

It is a promise by your Christ or awareness of being to your present conception of yourself that you will leave your present consciousness and appropriate another.

Man is such a slave to time that, if after he has appropriated a state of consciousness which is not now seen by the world and it, the appropriated state, does not immediately embody itself, he loses faith in his unseen claim; forthwith he drops it and returns to his former static state of being.

Because of this limitation of man, I have found it very helpful to employ a specified interval of time in making this journey into a prepared mansion.

"Wait but a little while" [Job 36:2].

We have all catalogued the different days of the week, months of the year and seasons. By this, I mean you and I have said time and again, "Why, today feels just like Sunday" or "-Monday" or "-Saturday". We have also said in the middle of Summer, "Why, this feels and looks like the Fall of the year".

This is positive proof that you and I have definite feelings associated with these different days, months and seasons of the year. Because of this association, we can at any time consciously dwell in that day or season which we have selected.

Do not selfishly define this interval in days and hours because you are anxious to receive it, but simply remain in the conviction that it is done—time, being purely relative, should be eliminated entirely—and your desire will be fulfilled.

This ability to dwell at any point in time permits us to employ time in our travel into the desired mansion.

Now I (consciousness) go to a point in time and there prepare a place. If I go to such a point in time and prepare a place, I shall return to this point in time where I have left; and I shall pick up and take you with me into that place which I have prepared, that where I AM, there ye may also be.

Let me give you an example of this travel.

Suppose you had an intense desire. Like most men who are enslaved by time, you might feel that you could not possibly realize so large a desire in a limited interval. But admitting that all things are possible to God, believing God to be the ME within you or your consciousness of being, you can say, "As John, I can do nothing; but since all things are possible to God and God I know to be my consciousness of being, I can realize my desire in a little while.

"How my desire will be realized I do not (as John) know, but by the very law of my being I do know that it shall be".

With this belief firmly established, decide what would be a relative, rational interval of time in which such a desire could be realized.

Again, let me remind you not to shorten the interval of time because you are anxious to receive your desire; make it a natural interval. No one can give you the time interval. Only you can say what the natural interval would be to you. The interval of time is relative, that is, no two individuals would give the same measurement of time for the realization of their desire.

Time is ever conditioned by man's conception of himself.

Confidence in yourself as determined by conditioned consciousness always shortens the interval of time.

If you were accustomed to great accomplishments, you would give yourself a much shorter interval in which to accomplish your desire than the man schooled in defeat.

If today were Wednesday and you decided that it would be quite possible for your desire to embody a new realization of yourself by Sunday, then Sunday becomes the point in time that you would visit.

To make this visit, you shut out Wednesday and let in Sunday. This is accomplished by simply feeling that it is Sunday. Begin to hear the church bells; begin to feel the quietness of the day and all that Sunday means to you; actually feel that it is Sunday.

When this is accomplished, feel the joy of having received that which on Wednesday was but a desire. Feel the complete thrill of having received it, and then return to Wednesday, the point in time you left behind you.

In doing this, you created a vacuum in consciousness by moving from Wednesday to Sunday. Nature, abhorring vacuums, rushes in to fill it, thereby fashioning a mould in the likeness of that which you potentially create, namely, the joy of having realized your defined desire.

As you return to Wednesday, you will be filled with a joyful expectancy, because you have established the consciousness of that which must take place the following Sunday.

As you walk through the interval of Thursday, Friday and Saturday, nothing disturbs you regardless of conditions, because you predetermined that which you would be on the Sabbath and that remains an unalterable conviction.

Having gone before and prepared the place, you have returned to John and are now taking him with you through the interval of three days into the prepared place that he might share your joy with you, *for where I AM, there ye may also be.*

] 16 [

THE TRIUNE GOD

And God said. Let Us make man in Our image, after Our likeness.

—Genesis 1:26

Having discovered God to be our awareness of being and this unconditioned changeless reality (the I AM) to be the only creator, let us see why the Bible records a trinity as the creator of the world.

In the 26th verse of the first chapter of Genesis, it is stated, "And God said, Let Us make man in Our image".

The churches refer to this plurality of Gods as God the Father, God the Son and God the Holy Spirit.

What is meant by "God the Father, God the Son and God the Holy Spirit" they have never attempted to explain for they are in the dark concerning this mystery.

The Father, Son and Holy Spirit are three aspects or conditions of the unconditioned awareness of being called God.

The consciousness of being precedes the consciousness of

being something. That unconditioned awareness which preceded all states of awareness is God—I AM.

The three conditioned aspects or divisions of itself can best be told in this manner:

The receptive attitude of mind is that aspect which receives impressions and therefore may be likened to a womb or Mother.

That which makes the impression is the male or pressing aspect and is therefore known as Father.

The impression in time becomes an expression, which expression is ever the likeness and image of the impression; therefore this objectified aspect is said to be the Son bearing witness of his Father-Mother.

An understanding of this mystery of the trinity enables the one who understands it to completely transform his world and fashion it to his own liking.

Here is a practical application of this mystery.

Sit quietly and decide what it is you would like most to express or possess. After you have decided, close your eyes and take your attention completely away from all that would deny the realization of the thing desired; then assume a receptive attitude of mind and play the game of supposing by imagining how you would feel if you were now to realize your desire.

Begin to listen as though space were talking to you and telling you that you are now that which you desire to be.

This receptive attitude is the state of consciousness that you must assume before an impression can be made.

As this pliable and impressive state of mind is attained, then begin to impress upon yourself the fact that you are that which you desired to be by claiming and feeling that you are now expressing and possessing that which you had decided to be and to have.

Continue in this attitude until the impression is made.

As you contemplate, being and possessing that which you have decided to be and to have, you will notice that with every inhalation of breath a joyful thrill courses through your entire being.

This thrill increases in intensity as you feel more and more the joy of being that which you are claiming yourself to be.

Then in one final deep inhalation, your whole being will explode with the joy of accomplishment and you will know by your feeling that you are impregnated by God, the Father.

As soon as the impression is made, open your eyes and return to the world that but a few moments before you had shut out.

In this receptive attitude of yours, while you contemplated being that which you desired to be, you were actually performing the spiritual act of generation so you are now on your return from this silent meditation a pregnant being bearing a child or impression, which child was immaculately conceived without the aid of man.

Doubt is the only force capable of disturbing the seed or impression; to avoid a miscarriage of so wonderful a child, walk in secrecy through the necessary interval of time that it will take the impression to become an expression.

Tell no man of your spiritual romance. Lock your secret within you in joy, confident and happy that some day you will bear the son of your lover by expressing and possessing the nature of your impression.

Then will you know the mystery of "God said. Let Us make man in Our image".

You will know that the plurality of Gods referred to is the three aspects of your own consciousness and that you are the trinity, meeting in a spiritual conclave to fashion a world in the image and likeness of that which you are conscious of being.

] 17 [

PRAYER

When thou prayest, enter into thy closet, and when thou hast shut thy door, pray to thy Father which is in secret; and thy Father which seeth in secret shall reward thee openly.

—MATTHEW 6:6

What things soever ye desire, when ye pray, believe that ye receive them, and ye shall have them.

—MARK 11:24

Prayer is the most wonderful experience man can have.

Unlike the daily murmurings of the vast majority of mankind in all lands who by their vain repetitions hope to gain the ear of God, prayer is the ecstasy of a spiritual wedding taking place in the deep, silent stillness of consciousness.

In its true sense prayer is God's marriage ceremony. Just as a maid on her wedding day relinquishes the name of her family to assume the name of her husband, in like manner, one who prays must relinquish his present name or nature and assume the nature of that for which he prays.

The gospels have clearly instructed man as to the performance of this ceremony in the following manner:

"When ye pray go within in secret and shut the door and your Father who sees in secret will reward you openly" [Matt. 6:6].

The going within is the entering of the bridal chamber. Just as no one but the bride and groom are permitted to enter so holy a room as the bridal suite on the night of the marriage ceremony, likewise no one but the one who prays and that for which he prays are permitted to enter the holy hour of prayer. As the bride and groom on entering the bridal suite securely shut the door against the outside world, so too must the one who enters the holy hour of prayer close the door of the senses and entirely shut out the world round about him.

This is accomplished by taking the attention completely away from all things other than that with which you are now in love (the thing desired).

The second phase of this spiritual ceremony is defined in these words, "When ye pray, believe that ye receive, and ye shall receive".

As you joyfully contemplate being and possessing that which you desire to be and to have, you have taken this second step and are therefore spiritually performing the acts of marriage and generation.

Your receptive attitude of mind while praying or contemplating can be likened to a bride or womb for it is that aspect of mind which receives the impressions.

That which you contemplate being is the groom, for it is the name or nature you assume and therefore is that which leaves its impregnation; so one dies to maidenhood or present nature as one assumes the name and nature of the impregnation.

Lost in contemplation and having assumed the name and

nature of the thing contemplated, your whole being thrills with the joy of being it. This thrill, which runs through your entire being as you appropriate the consciousness of your desire, is the proof that you are both married and impregnated.

As you return from this silent meditation, the door is once more opened upon the world you had left behind. But this time you return as a pregnant bride.

You enter the world a changed being and, although no one but you knows of this wonderful romance, the world will, in a very short while, see the signs of your pregnancy, for you will begin to express that which you in your hour of silence felt yourself to be.

The mother of the world or bride of the Lord is purposely called Mary, or water, for water loses its identity as it assumes the nature of that with which it is mixed; likewise, Mary, the receptive attitude of mind, must lose its identity as it assumes the nature of the thing desired.

Only as one is willing to give up his present limitations and identity can he become that which he desires to be.

Prayer is the formula by which such divorces and marriages are accomplished. *"Two shall agree as touching anything and it shall be established on earth"* [Matt. 18:19].

The two agreeing are you, the bride, and the thing desired, the groom.

As this agreement is accomplished, a son bearing witness of this union will be born. You begin to express and possess that which you are conscious of being.

Praying, then, is recognizing yourself to be that which you desire to be rather than begging God for that which you desire.

Millions of prayers are daily unanswered because man prays to a God who does not exist.

Consciousness being God, one must seek in consciousness for the thing desired by assuming the consciousness of the quality desired. Only as one does this will his prayers be answered.

To be conscious of being poor while praying for riches is to be rewarded with that which you are conscious of being, namely, poverty.

Prayers, to be successful, must be claimed and appropriated. Assume the positive consciousness of the thing desired.

With your desire defined, quietly go within and shut the door behind you. Lose yourself in your desire; feel yourself to be one with it; remain in this fixation until you have absorbed the life and name by claiming and feeling yourself to be and to have that which you desired.

When you emerge from the hour of prayer, you must do so conscious of being and possessing that which you heretofore desired.

THE TWELVE DISCIPLES

And when He had called unto Him His twelve disciples. He gave them power against unclean spirits, to cast them out, and to heal all manner of sickness and all manner of disease.

—MATTHEW 10:1

The twelve disciples represent the twelve qualities of mind which can be controlled and disciplined by man.

If disciplined, they will at all times obey the command of the one who has disciplined them.

These twelve qualities in man are potentials of every mind. Undisciplined, their actions resemble more the actions of a mob than they do of a trained and disciplined army. All the storms and confusions that engulf man can be traced directly to these twelve ill-related characteristics of the human mind in its present slumbering state.

Until they are awakened and disciplined, they will permit every rumor and sensuous emotion to move them.

When these twelve are disciplined and brought under control, the one who accomplishes this control will say to them,

"Hereafter I call you not slaves, but friends" *["Henceforth I call you not servants for the servant knoweth not what his lord doeth but I have called you friends, for all things that I have heard of My Father I have made known unto you"* (John 15:15)*].*

He knows that from that moment on, each acquired disciplined attribute of mind will befriend and protect him.

The names of the twelve qualities reveal their natures.

These names are not given to them until they are called to discipleship.

They are: Simon, who was later surnamed Peter, Andrew, James, John, Philip, Bartholomew, Thomas, Matthew, James the son of Alphaeus, Thaddaeus, Simon the Canaanite and Judas [Matt. 10; Mark 1: Mark 3; Luke 6].

The first quality to be called and disciplined is Simon, or the attribute of hearing.

This faculty, when lifted to the level of a disciple, permits only such impressions to reach consciousness as those which his hearing has commanded him to let enter. No matter what the wisdom of man might suggest or the evidence of his senses convey, if such suggestions and ideas are not in keeping with that which he hears, he remains unmoved. This one has been instructed by his Lord and made to understand that every suggestion he permits to pass his gate will, on reaching his Lord and Master (his consciousness), leave its impression there, which impression must in time become an expression.

The instruction to Simon is that he should permit only dignified and honorable visitors or impressions to enter the house (consciousness) of his Lord. No mistake can be covered up or hidden from his Master, for every expression of life tells his Lord whom he consciously or unconsciously entertained.

When Simon, by his works, proves himself to be a true and

faithful disciple, then he receives the surname of Peter, or the rock, the unmoved disciple, the one who cannot be bribed or coerced by any visitor. He is called by his Lord Simon Peter, the one who faithfully hears the commands of his Lord and besides which commands he hears not.

It is this Simon Peter who discovers the I AM to be Christ, and for his discovery is given the keys to heaven, and is made the foundation stone upon which the Temple of God rests.

Buildings must have firm foundations and only the disciplined hearing can, on learning that the I AM is Christ, remain firm and unmoved in the knowledge that I AM Christ and beside ME there is no savior.

The second quality to be called to discipleship is Andrew, or courage.

As the first quality, faith in oneself, is developed, it automatically calls into being its brother, courage.

Faith in oneself, which asks no man's help but quietly and alone appropriates the consciousness of the quality desired and—in spite of reason or the evidence of his senses to the contrary continues faithful-patiently waiting in the knowledge that his unseen claim if sustained must be realized—such faith develops a courage and strength of character that are beyond the wildest dreams of the undisciplined man whose faith is in things seen.

The faith of the undisciplined man cannot really be called faith. For if the armies, medicines or wisdom of man in which his faith is placed be taken from him, his faith and courage go with it. But from the disciplined one the whole world could be taken and yet he would remain faithful in the knowledge that the state of consciousness in which he abides must in due season embody itself. This courage is Peter's brother Andrew, the disciple, who knows what it is to dare, to do and to be silent.

The next two (third & fourth) who are called are also related.

These are the brothers, James and John, James the just, the righteous judge, and his brother John, the beloved.

Justice to be wise must be administered with love, ever turning the other cheek and at all times returning good for evil, love for hate, non-violence for violence.

The disciple James, symbol of a disciplined judgment, must, when raised to the high office of a supreme judge, be blindfolded that he may not be influenced by the flesh nor judge after the appearances of being. Disciplined judgment is administered by one who is not influenced by appearances.

The one who has called these brothers to discipleship continues faithful to his command to hear only that which he has been commanded to hear, namely, the Good.

The man who has this quality of his mind disciplined is incapable of hearing and accepting as true anything—either of himself or another—which does not on the hearing fill his heart with love.

These two disciples or aspects of the mind are one and inseparable when awakened.

Such a disciplined one forgives all men for being that which they are. He knows as a wise judge that every man perfectly expresses that which he is, as man, conscious of being.

He knows that upon the changeless foundation of consciousness all manifestation rests, that changes of expression can be brought about only through changes of consciousness.

With neither condemnation nor criticism, these disciplined qualities of the mind permit everyone to be that which he is.

However, although allowing this perfect freedom of choice to all, they are nevertheless ever watchful to see that they themselves prophesy and do—both for others and themselves— only such things which when expressed glorify, dignify and give joy to the expresser.

The fifth quality called to discipleship is Philip.

This one asked to be shown the Father. The awakened man knows that the Father is the state of consciousness in which man dwells, and that this state or Father can be seen only as it is expressed.

He knows himself to be the perfect likeness or image of that consciousness with which he is identified.

So He declares, "No man has at any time seen My Father; but I, the Son, who dwelleth in His bosom have revealed Him; *["No one has seen God at any time; the only begotten God who is in the bosom of the Father, He has explained Him"* (John 1:18)*]*; therefore, when you see Me, the Son, you see My Father, for I come to bear witness of My Father" *["If ye had known Me, ye should have known My Father also: and from henceforth ye know Him, and have seen Him"* (John 14:7); *"Have I been so long time with you, and yet hast thou not known Me, Philip? he that hath seen Me hath seen the Father; and how sayest thou then, Shew us the Father? Believest thou not that I am in the Father, and the Father in Me? the words that I speak unto you I speak not of Myself: but the Father that dwelleth in Me, He doeth the works. Believe Me that I am in the Father, and the Father in Me: or else believe Me for the very works' sake* (John 14:9–11)*]*.

I and My Father, consciousness and its expression, God and man, are one.

This aspect of the mind, when disciplined, persists until ideas, ambitions and desires become embodied realities. This is the quality which states "Yet in my flesh shall I see God" [Job 19:26].

It knows how to make the word flesh [John 1:14], how to give form to the formless. The sixth disciple is called Bartholomew.

This quality is the imaginative faculty, which quality of the mind when once awake distinguishes one from the masses.

An awakened imagination places the one so awakened head and shoulders above the average man, giving him the appearance of a beacon light in a world of darkness.

No quality so separates man from man as does the disciplined imagination.

This is the separation of the wheat from the chaff. Those who have given most to Society are our artists, scientists, inventors and others with vivid imaginations.

Should a survey be made to determine the reason why so many seemingly educated men and women fail in their after-college years or should it be made to determine the reason for the different earning powers of the masses, there would be no doubt but that imagination played the important part.

Such a survey would show that it is imagination which makes one a leader while the lack of it makes one a follower.

Instead of developing the imagination of man, our educational system oftentimes stifles it by attempting to put into the mind of man the wisdom he seeks. It forces him to memorize a number of text books which, all too soon, are disproved by later text books.

Education is not accomplished by putting something into man; its purpose is to draw out of man the wisdom which is latent within him. May the reader call Bartholomew to discipleship, for only as this quality is raised to discipleship will you have the capacity to conceive ideas that will lift you beyond the limitations of man.

The seventh is called Thomas.

This disciplined quality doubts or denies every rumor and suggestion that are not in harmony with that which Simon Peter has been commanded to let enter.

The man who is conscious of being healthy (not because of inherited health, diets or climate, but because he is awakened and knows the state of consciousness in which he lives) will, in spite of the conditions of the world, continue to express health.

He could hear, through the press, radio and wise men of the world that a plague was sweeping the earth and yet he would remain unmoved and unimpressed. Thomas, the doubter—when disciplined—would deny that sickness or anything else which was not in sympathy with the consciousness to which he belonged had any power to affect him.

This quality of denial—when disciplined—protects man from receiving impressions that are not in harmony with his nature. He adopts an attitude of total indifference to all suggestions that are foreign to that which he desires to express. Disciplined denial is not a fight or a struggle but total indifference.

Matthew, the eighth, is the gift of God.

This quality of the mind reveals man's desires as gifts of God.

The man who has called this disciple into being knows that every desire of his heart is a gift from heaven and that it contains both the power and the plan of its self-expression.

Such a man never questions the manner of its expression.

He knows that the plan of expression is never revealed to man for God's ways are past finding out [Rom. 11:33].

He fully accepts his desires as gifts already received and goes his way in peace confident that they shall appear.

The ninth disciple is called James, the son of Alphaeus.

This is the quality of discernment. A clear and ordered mind is the voice which calls this disciple into being.

This faculty perceives that which is not revealed to the eye of man. This disciple judges not from appearances for it has the capacity to function in the realm of causes and so is never misled by appearances.

Clairvoyance is the faculty which is awakened when this quality is developed and disciplined, not the clairvoyance of the mediumistic séance rooms, but the true clairvoyance or clear seeing of the mystic. That is, this aspect of the mind has the capacity to interpret that which is seen. Discernment or the capacity to diagnose is the quality of James the son of Alphaeus.

Thaddaeus, the tenth, is the disciple of praise, a quality in which the undisciplined man is woefully lacking.

When this quality of praise and thanksgiving is awake within man, he walks with the words, "Thank you, Father", ever on his lips.

He knows that his thanks for things not seen opens the windows of heaven and permits gifts beyond his capacity to receive to be poured upon him.

The man who is not thankful for things received is not likely to be the recipient of many gifts from the same source.

Until this quality of the mind is disciplined, man will not see the desert blossom as the rose. Praise and thanksgiving are to the invisible gifts of God (one's desires) what rain and sun are to the unseen seeds in the bosom of the earth.

The eleventh quality called is Simon of Canaan.

A good key phrase for this disciple is "Hearing good news". Simon of Canaan, or Simon from the land of milk and honey, when called to discipleship, is proof that the one who calls this faculty into being has become conscious of the abundant life. He can say with the Psalmist David, "Thou preparest a table before me in the presence of mine enemies; thou anointest my head with oil; my cup runneth over" [Ps. 23:5]. This disciplined aspect of the mind is incapable of hearing anything other than good news and so is well qualified to preach the Gospel or Good-spell.

The twelfth and last of the disciplined qualities of the mind is called Judas.

When this quality is awake, man knows that he must die to that which he is before he can become that which he desires to be.

So it is said of this disciple that he committed suicide, which is the mystic's way of telling the initiated that Judas is the disciplined aspect of detachment.

This one knows that his I AM or consciousness is his savior, so he lets all other saviors go.

This quality—when disciplined—gives one the strength to let go.

The man who has called Judas into being has learned how to take his attention away from problems or limitations and to place it upon that which is the solution or savior.

"Except ye be born again, you cannot in anywise enter the Kingdom of Heaven" ["Truly, truly, I say to you, unless one is born again, he cannot see the kingdom of God" (John 3:3)]. "No greater love hath man than this, that he give his life for a friend" [*"Greater love hath no man than this, that a man lay down his life for his friends"* (John 15:13)].

When man realizes that the quality desired, if realized, would save and befriend him, he willingly gives up his life (present conception of himself) for his friend by detaching his consciousness from that which he is conscious of being and assuming the consciousness of that which he desires to be.

Judas, the one whom the world in its ignorance has blackened, will, when man awakes from his undisciplined state, be placed on high for God is love and no greater love has a man than this—that he lay down his life for a friend.

Until man lets go of that which he is now conscious of being, he will not become that which he desires to be; and Judas is the one who accomplishes this through suicide or detachment.

These are the twelve qualities which were given to man in the foundation of the world.

Man's duty is to raise them to the level of discipleship. When this is accomplished, man will say, "I have finished the work which thou gavest Me to do. I have glorified Thee on earth and now, o, Father, glorify Thou Me with Thine own Self with the glory which I had with Thee before the world was" [John 17:4, 5].

] 19 [

LIQUID LIGHT

In Him we live and move, and have our being.

—ACTS 17:28

Psychically, this world appears as an ocean of light containing within itself all things, including man, as pulsating bodies enveloped in liquid light.

The Biblical story of the Flood [Gen. 6–8] is the state in which man lives.

Man is actually inundated in an ocean of liquid light in which countless numbers of light-beings move.

The story of the Flood is really being enacted today.

Man is the Ark containing within himself the male-female principles of every living thing.

The dove or idea which is sent out to find dry land is man's attempt to embody his ideas. Man's ideas resemble birds in flight—like the dove in the story, returning to man without finding a place to rest.

If man will not let such fruitless searches discourage him, one day the bird will return with a green sprig. After assuming the consciousness of the thing desired, he will be convinced that it is so; and he will feel and know that he is that which he has consciously appropriated, even though it is not yet confirmed by his senses.

One day man will become so identified with his conception that he will know it to be himself, and he will declare, "I AM; I AM that which I desire to be (I AM that I AM)". He will find that, as he does so, he will begin to embody his desire (the dove or desire will this time find dry land), thereby realizing the mystery of the word made flesh.

Everything in the world is a crystallization of this liquid light. "I AM the light of the world" [John 8:12; John 9:5; John 12:46].

Your awareness of being is the liquid light of the world, which crystallizes into the conceptions you have of yourself.

Your unconditioned awareness of being first conceived itself in liquid light (which is the initial velocity of the universe). All things, from the highest to the lowest vibrations or expressions of life, are nothing more than the different vibrations of velocities of this initial velocity; gold, silver, iron, wood, flesh etc., are only different expressions or velocities of this one substance-liquid light.

All things are crystallized liquid light; the differentiation or infinity of expression is caused by the conceiver's desire to know himself.

Your conception of yourself automatically determines the velocity necessary to express that which you have conceived yourself to be.

The world is an ocean of liquid light in countless different states of crystallization.

] 20 [

THE BREATH OF LIFE

Then the LORD God formed man of dust from the ground, and breathed into his nostrils the breath of life; and man became a living being.

—GENESIS 2:7

As thou knowest not what is the way of the spirit, nor how the bones do grow in the womb of her that is with child: even so thou knowest not the works of God who maketh all Just as you don't know how the breath of life enters the limbs of a child within its mother's womb, you also don't understand how God, who made everything, works.

—ECCLESIASTES 11:5

And it came to pass after these things, that the son of the woman, the mistress of the house, fell sick; and his sickness was so sore, that there was no breath left in him.

—1 KINGS 17:17

And he (Elisha) went up, and lay upon the child, and put his mouth upon his mouth, and his eyes upon his eyes, and his hands upon his hands: and stretched himself upon the child; and the flesh of the child waxed warm.

—2 KINGS 4:34

But after the three and a half days, the breath of life from God came into them, and they stood on their feet; and great fear fell upon those who were watching them.

—REVELATION 11:11

D id the Prophet Elijah *[and or Elisha]* really restore to life the dead child of the Widow?

This story, along with all the other stories of the Bible, is a psychological drama which takes place in the consciousness of man.

The Widow symbolizes every man and woman in the world; the dead child represents the frustrated desires and ambitions of man; while the prophet, Elijah *[and or Elisha]*, symbolizes the God power within man, or man's awareness of being.

The story tells us that the prophet took the dead child from the Widow's bosom and carried him into an upper room. As he entered this upper room he closed the door behind them; placing the child upon a bed, he breathed life into him; returning to the mother, he gave her the child and said, "Woman, thy son liveth" *["See, thy son liveth"* (1 Kings 17:23; 2 Kings 4:36)*].*

Man's desires can be symbolized as the dead child.

The mere fact that he desires is positive proof that the thing desired is not yet a living reality in his world.

He tries in every conceivable way to nurse this desire into

reality, to make it live, but finds in the end that all attempts are fruitless.

Most men are not aware of the existence of the infinite power within themselves as the prophet.

They remain indefinitely with a dead child in their arms, not realizing that the desire is the positive indication of limitless capacities for its fulfillment.

Let man once recognize that his consciousness is a prophet who breathes life into all that he is conscious of being, and he will close the door of his senses against his problem and fix his attention—solely on that which he desires, knowing that by so doing, his desires are certain to be realized.

He will discover recognition to be the breath of life, for he will perceive—as he consciously claims himself to be now expressing or possessing all he desires to be or to have—that he will be breathing the breath *[sic!]* of life into his desire.

The quality claimed for the desire (in a way unknown to him) will begin to move and become a living reality in his world.

Yes, the Prophet Elijah *[and/or Elisha]* lives forever as man's limitless consciousness of being, the widow as his limited consciousness of being and the child as that which he desires to be.

21

DANIEL IN THE LIONS' DEN

Thy God whom thou servest continually: He will deliver thee.

—DANIEL 6:16

The story of Daniel is the story of every man. It is recorded that Daniel, while locked in the lions' den, turned his back upon the hungry beasts; and with his vision turned toward the light coming from above, he prayed to the one and only God. The lions, who were purposely starved for the feast, remained powerless to hurt the prophet. Daniel's faith in God was so great that it finally brought about his freedom and his appointment to a high office in the government of his country [Dan. 6:13–28].

This story was written for you to instruct you in the art of freeing yourself from any problem or prison in the world.

Most of us on finding ourselves in the lions' den would be concerned only with the lions, we would not be thinking of any other problem in the whole wide world but that of lions; yet we are told that Daniel turned his back upon them and looked toward the light that was God. If we could follow the example of Daniel while threatened with any dire disaster such as lions, poverty or sickness, if, like Daniel, we could remove our attention to the light that is God, our solutions would be similarly simple.

For example, if you were imprisoned, no man would need to tell you that what you should desire is freedom. Freedom or rather the desire to be free would be automatic.

The same would be true if you found yourself sick or in debt or in any other predicament.

Lions represent seemingly unsoluble situations of a threatening nature.

Every problem automatically produces its solution in the form of a desire to be free from the problem.

Therefore, turn your back upon your problem and focus your attention upon the desired solution by already feeling yourself to be that which you desire.

Continue in this belief, and you will find that your prison wall will disappear as you begin to express that which you have become conscious of being.

I have seen people, apparently hopelessly in debt, apply this principle, and, in but a very short time, debts that were mountainous were removed. I have also seen those whom doctors had given up as uncurable apply this principle and, in an incredibly short time, their so-called incurable disease vanished and left no scar.

Look upon your desires as the spoken words of God and every word of prophecy of that which you are capable of being. Do not question whether you are worthy or unworthy to realize these desires. Accept them as they come to you. Give thanks for them as though they were gifts. Feel happy and grateful for having received such wonderful gifts. Then go your way in peace.

Such simple acceptance of your desires is like the dropping of fertile seed into an ever-prepared soil.

When you drop your desire in consciousness as a seed, confident that it shall appear in its full-blown potential, you have done all that is expected of you. To be worried or concerned about the manner of their unfoldment is to hold these fertile seeds in a mental grasp and, therefore, to prevent them from really maturing to full harvest.

Don't be anxious or concerned as to results. Results will follow just as surely as day follows night.

Have faith in this planting until the evidence is manifest to you that it is so. Your confidence in this procedure will pay great rewards. You wait but a little while in the consciousness of the thing desired; then suddenly, and when you least expect it, the thing felt becomes your expression. Life is no respecter of persons [Acts 10:34; Rom. 2:11] and destroys nothing; it continues to keep alive that which man is conscious of being.

Things will disappear only as man changes his consciousness. Deny it if you will, it still remains a fact that consciousness is the only reality and things but mirror that which you are conscious of being.

The heavenly state you seek will be found only in consciousness for the Kingdom of Heaven is within you.

Your consciousness is the only living reality, the eternal head of creation. That which you are conscious of being is the temporal body that you wear.

To turn your attention from that which you are aware of being is to decapitate that body; but, just as a chicken or snake continues to jump and throb for a while after its head has been removed, likewise qualities and conditions appear to live for a while after your attention has been taken from them.

Man, not knowing this law of consciousness, constantly gives thought to his previous habitual conditions and, through being attentive to them, places upon these dead bodies the eternal head of creation; thereby he reanimates and re-resurrects them.

You must leave these dead bodies alone and *let the dead bury the dead* [Matt. 8:22; Luke 9:60].

Man, having put his hand to the plough (that is, after assuming the consciousness of the quality desired), by looking back, can only defeat his fitness for the Kingdom of Heaven [Luke 9:62].

As the will of heaven is ever done on earth, you are today in the heaven that you have established within yourself, for here on this very earth your heaven reveals itself.

The Kingdom of Heaven really is at hand. Now is the accepted time. So create a new heaven, enter into a new state of consciousness and a new earth will appear.

22

FISHING

They went forth, and entered into a ship, and that night they caught nothing.

—JOHN 21:3

And He said unto them, Cast the net on the right side of the ship, and ye shall find. They cast therefore, and now they were not able to draw it for the multitude of fishes.

—JOHN 21:6

I t is recorded that the disciples fished all night and caught nothing. Then Jesus appeared upon the scene and told them to cast their nets again, but, this time, to cast them on the right side. Peter obeyed the voice of Jesus and cast his nets once more into the waters. Where but a moment before the water was completely empty of fish, the nets almost broke with the number of the resulting catch [John 21:3–6].

Man, fishing all through the night of human ignorance, attempts to realize his desires through effort and struggle only to find in the end that his search is fruitless. When man discovers his awareness of being to be Christ Jesus, he will obey its voice and let it direct his fishing. He will cast his hook on the right side; he will apply the law in the right manner and will seek in consciousness for the thing desired. Finding it there, he will know that it will be multiplied in the world of form.

Those who have had the pleasure of fishing know what a thrill it is to feel the fish upon the hook. The bite of the fish is followed by the play of the fish; this play, in turn, is followed by the landing of the fish.

Something similar takes place in the consciousness of man as he fishes for the manifestations of life.

Fishermen know that if they wish to catch big fish, they must fish in deep waters; if you would catch a large measure of life, you must leave behind you the shallow waters with its many reefs and barriers and launch out into the deep blue waters where the big ones play.

To catch the large manifestations of life you must enter into deeper and freer states of consciousness; only in these depths do the big expressions of life live.

Here is a simple formula for successful fishing.

First, decide what it is you want to express or possess. This is essential.

You must definitely know what you want of life before you can fish for it. After your decision is made, turn from the world of sense, remove your attention from the problem and place it on just being, by repeating quietly but with feeling, "I AM".

As your attention is removed from the world round about you and placed upon the I AM, so that you are lost in the feeling of simply being, you will find yourself slipping the anchor that tied you to the shallows of your problem; and effortlessly you will find yourself moving out into the deep.

The sensation which accompanies this act is one of expansion. You will feel yourself rise and expand as though you were actually growing. Do not be afraid of this floating, growing experience for you are not going to die to anything but your limitations.

However, your limitations are going to die as you move away from them for they live only in your consciousness.

In this deep or expanded consciousness, you will feel yourself to be a mighty pulsating power as deep and as rhythmical as the ocean. This expanded feeling is the signal that you are now in the deep blue waters where the big fish swim. Suppose the fish you decided to catch were health and freedom; you begin to fish in this formless pulsating depth of yourself for these qualities or states of consciousness by feeling "I AM healthy"—"I AM free".

You continue claiming and feeling yourself to be healthy and free until the conviction that you are so possesses you.

As the conviction is born within you, so that all doubts pass away and you know and feel that you are free from the limitations of the past, you will know that you have hooked these fish.

The joy which courses through your entire being on feeling that you are that which you desired to be is equal to the thrill of the fisherman as he hooks his fish.

Now comes the play of the fish. This is accomplished by returning to the world of the senses.

As you open your eyes on the world round about you, the conviction and the consciousness that you are healthy and free should be so established within you that your whole being thrills in anticipation.

Then, as you walk through the necessary interval of time that it will take the things felt to embody themselves, you will feel a secret thrill in knowing that in a little while that which no man sees, but that which you feel and know that you are, will be landed.

In a moment when you think not, while you faithfully walk in this consciousness, you will begin to express and possess that which you are conscious of being and possessing; experiencing with the fisherman the joy of landing the big one.

Now, go and fish for the manifestations of life by casting your nets in the right side.

23

BE EARS THAT HEAR

Let these sayings sink down into your ears: For the Son of Man shall be delivered into the hands of men.

—LUKE 9:44

"Let these sayings sink down into your ears, for the Son of Man shall be delivered into the hands of men". Be not as those who have eyes that see not and ears that hear not.

Let these revelations sink deep into your ears, for after the Son (idea) is conceived, man with his false values (reason) will attempt to explain the why and wherefore of the Son's expression, and in so doing, will rend him to pieces.

After men have agreed that a certain thing is humanly impossible and therefore cannot be done, let someone accomplish the impossible thing; the wise ones who said it could not be done will begin to tell you why and how it happened. After they are all through tearing the seamless robe [John 19:23] (cause of manifestation) apart, they will be as far from the truth as they were when they proclaimed it impossible. As long as man looks for the cause of expression in places other than the expresser, he looks in vain.

For thousands of years, man has been told, "I AM the resurrection and the life" [John 11:25]. "No manifestation cometh unto me save I draw it" [John 6:44], but man will not believe it.

He prefers to believe in causes outside of himself.

The moment that which was not seen becomes seen, man is ready to explain the cause and purpose of its appearance.

Thus, the Son of Man (idea desiring manifestation) is constantly being destroyed at the hands of (reasonable explanation or wisdom) man.

Now that your awareness is revealed to you as cause of all expression, do not return to the darkness of Egypt with its many gods. There is but one God. The one and only God is your awareness.

"And all the inhabitants of the earth are reputed as nothing. And He doeth according to His will in the army of Heaven, and among the inhabitants of the earth and none can stay His hand, or say unto him what doest Thou?" *["All the inhabitants of the earth are accounted as nothing, But He does according to His will in the host of heaven And among the inhabitants of earth: And no one can ward off His hand Or say to Him. 'What have You done?'"* (Dan. 4:35)].

If the whole world should agree that a certain thing could not be expressed and yet you became aware of being that which they had agreed could not be expressed, you would express it.

Your awareness never asks permission to express that which you are aware of being. It does so, naturally and without effort, in spite of the wisdom of man and all opposition.

"Salute no man by the way" *["Carry no money belt, no bag,*

no shoes; and greet no one on the way" (Luke 10:4; 2 Kings 4:29)].

This is not a command to be insolent or unfriendly, but a reminder not to recognize a superior, not to see in anyone a barrier to your expression.

None can stay your hand or question your ability to express that which you are conscious of being.

Do not judge after the appearances of a thing, "for all are as nothing in the eyes of God" [*"All the nations are as nothing before Him, They are regarded by Him as less than nothing and meaningless"* (Isa. 40:17)].

When the disciples through their judgment of appearances saw the insane child [Mark 9:17–29; Luke 9:37–43], they thought it a more difficult problem to solve than others they had seen; and so they failed to achieve a cure.

In judging after appearances, they forgot that all things were possible to God [Matt. 19:26; Mark 10:27].

Hypnotized as they were by the reality of appearances, they could not feel the naturalness of sanity.

The only way for you to avoid such failures is to constantly bear in mind that your awareness is the Almighty, the all-wise presence; without help, this unknown presence within you effortlessly outpictures that which you are aware of being.

Be perfectly indifferent to the evidence of the senses, so that you may feel the naturalness of your desire, and your desire will be realized.

Turn from appearances and feel the naturalness of that perfect perception within yourself, a quality never to be distrusted or doubted. Its understanding will never lead you astray.

Your desire is the solution of your problem. As the desire is realized, the problem is dissolved.

You cannot force anything outwardly by the mightiest effort of the will. There is only one way you can command the things you want and that is by assuming the consciousness of the things desired.

There is a vast difference between feeling a thing and merely knowing it intellectually.

You must accept without reservation the fact that by possessing (feeling) a thing in consciousness, you have commanded the reality that causes it to come into existence in concrete form.

You must be absolutely convinced of an unbroken connection between the invisible reality and its visible manifestation. Your inner acceptance must become an intense, unalterable conviction which transcends both reason and intellect, renouncing entirely any belief in the reality of the externalization except as a reflection of an inner state of consciousness. When you really understand and believe these things, you will have built up so profound a certainty that nothing can shake you.

Your desires are the invisible realities which respond only to the commands of God. God commands the invisible to appear by claiming himself to be the thing commanded. "He made Himself equal with God and found it not robbery to do the works of God" [Phil. 2:6].

Now let this saying sink deep in your ear: BE CONSCIOUS OF BEING THAT WHICH YOU WANT TO APPEAR.

] 24 [

CLAIRVOYANCE

Having eyes, see ye not? and having ears,
hear ye not? and do ye not remember?

—MARK 8:18

True clairvoyance rests, not in your ability to see things beyond the range of human vision, but rather in your ability to understand that which you see.

A financial statement can be seen by anyone, but very few can read a financial statement. The capacity to interpret the statement is the mark of clear seeing or clairvoyance.

That every object, both animate and inanimate, is enveloped in a liquid light which moves and pulsates with an energy far more radiant than the objects themselves, no one knows better than the author; but he also knows that the ability to see such auras is not equal to the ability to understand that which one sees in the world around about him.

To illustrate this point, here is a story with which the whole world is familiar, yet only the true mystic or clairvoyant has ever really seen it.

Synopsis

The story of Dumas' "Count of Monte Cristo" is, to the mystic and true clairvoyant, the biography of every man.

I

Edmond Dantés, a young sailor, finds the captain of his ship dead. Taking command of the ship in the midst of a storm-swept sea, he attempts to steer the ship into a safe anchorage.

Commentary
Life itself is a storm-swept sea with which man wrestles as he tries to steer himself into a haven of rest.

II

On Dantés is a secret document which must be given to a man he does not know, but who will make himself known to the young sailor in due time. This document is a plan to set the Emperor Napoleon free from his prison on the Isle of Elba.

Commentary
Within every man is the secret plan that will set free the mighty emperor within himself.

III

As Dantés reaches port, three men (who by their flattery and praise have succeeded in worming their way into the good graces of the present king), fearing any change that would alter their positions in the government, have the young mariner arrested and committed to the catacombs.

Commentary

Man in his attempt to find security in this world is misled by the false lights of greed, vanity and power.

Most men believe that fame, great wealth or political power would secure them against the storms of life. So they seek to acquire these as the anchors of their life, only to find that in their search for these they gradually lose the knowledge of their true being. If man places his faith in things other than himself, that in which his faith is placed, will in time destroy him; at which time he will be as one imprisoned in confusion and despair.

IV

Here in this tomb. Dantés is forgotten and left to rot. Many years pass. Then one day, Dantés (who is by this time a living skeleton) hears a knock on his wall. Answering this knock, he hears the voice of one on the other side of the stone. In response to this voice, Dantés removes the stone and discovers an old priest who has been in prison so long that no one knows the reason for his imprisonment or the length of time he has been there.

Commentary

Here behind these walls of mental darkness, man remains in what appears to be a living death. After years of disappointment, man turns from these false friends, and he discovers within himself the ancient one (his awareness of being) who has been buried since the day he first believed himself to be man and forgot that he was God.

V

The old priest had spent many years digging his way out of this living tomb only to discover that he had dug his way into Dantés' tomb. He then resigns himself to his fate and decides to find his joy and freedom by instructing Dantés in all that he knows concerning the mysteries of life and to aid him to escape as well.

Dantés, at first, is impatient to acquire all this information; but the old priest, with infinite patience garnered through his long imprisonment, shows Dantés how unfit he is to receive this knowledge in his present, unprepared, anxious mind. So, with philosophic calm, he slowly reveals to the young man the mysteries of life and time.

Commentary

This revelation is so wonderful that when man first hears it he wants to acquire it all at once; but he finds that, after numberless years spent in the belief of being man, he has so completely forgotten his true identity that he is now incapable of absorbing this memory all at once. He also discovers that he can do so only in proportion to his letting go of all human values and opinions.

VI

As Dantés ripens under the old priest's instructions, the old man finds himself living more and more in the consciousness of Dantés. Finally, he imparts his last bit of wisdom to Dantés, making him competent to handle positions of trust. He then tells him of an inexhaustible treasure buried on the Isle of Monte Cristo.

Commentary

As man drops these cherished human values, he absorbs more and more of the light (the old priest), until finally he becomes the light and knows himself to be the ancient one. *I AM the light of the world.*

VII

At this revelation, the walls of the catacomb which separated them from the ocean above cave in, crushing the old man to death. The guards, discovering the accident, sew the old priest's body into a sack and prepare to cast it out to sea. As they leave to get a stretcher, Dantés removes the body of the old priest and sews himself into the bag. The guards, unaware of this change of bodies, and believing him to be the old man, throw Dantés into the water.

Commentary

The flowing of both blood and water in the death of the old priest is comparable to the flow of blood and water from the side of Jesus as the Roman soldiers pierced him, the phenomenon which always takes place at birth (here symbolizing the birth of a higher consciousness).

VIII

Dantés frees himself from the sack, goes to the Isle of Monte Cristo and discovers the buried treasure. Then, armed with this fabulous wealth and this superhuman wisdom, he discards his human identity of Edmond Dantés and assumes the title of the Count of Monte Cristo.

Commentary
Man discovers his awareness of being to be the inexhaustible treasure of the universe. In that day, when man makes this discovery, he dies as man and awakes as God.

Yes, Edmond Dantés becomes the Count of Monte Cristo. Man becomes Christ.

25

TWENTY-THIRD PSALM

I

The Lord is my Shepherd; I shall not want.

Commentary

My awareness is my Lord and Shepherd. That which I AM aware of being is the sheep that follow me. So good a shepherd is my awareness of being, it has never lost one sheep or thing that I AM aware of being.

My consciousness is a voice calling in the wilderness of human confusion; calling all that I AM conscious of being to follow me.

So well do my sheep know my voice, they have never failed to respond to my call; nor will there come a time when that which I am convinced that I AM will fail to find me.

I AM an open door for all that I AM to enter.

My awareness of being is Lord and Shepherd of my life. Now I know I shall never be in need of proof or lack the evidence of that which I am aware of being. Knowing this, I shall become aware of being great, loving, wealthy, healthy and all other attributes that I admire.

II

He maketh me to lie down in green pastures.

Commentary
My awareness of being magnifies all that I am aware of being, so there is ever an abundance of that which I am conscious of being.

It makes no difference what it is that man is conscious of being, he will find it eternally springing in his world.

The Lord's measure (man's conception of himself) is always pressed down, shaken together and running over.

III

He leadeth me beside the still waters.

Commentary
There is no need to fight for that which I am conscious of being, for all that I am conscious of being shall be led to me as effortlessly as a shepherd leads his flock to the still waters of a quiet spring.

IV

He restoreth my soul; He leadeth me in the paths of righteousness for His Name's sake.

Commentary
Now that my memory is restored—so that I know I AM the Lord and beside me there is no God—my kingdom is restored.

My kingdom—which became dismembered in the day that I believed in powers apart from myself—is now fully restored.

Now that I know my awareness of being is God, I shall make the right use of this knowledge by becoming aware of being that which I desire to be.

V

Yea, though I walk through the valley of the shadow of death, I will fear no evil; for Thou art with me; Thy rod and Thy staff, they comfort me.

Commentary

Yes, though I walk through all the confusion and changing opinions of men, I will fear no evil, for I have found consciousness to be that which makes the confusion. Having in my own case restored it to its rightful place and dignity, I shall, in spite of the confusion, outpicture that which I am now conscious of being. And the very confusion will echo and reflect my own dignity.

VI

Thou preparest a table before me in the presence of mine enemies; Thou anointest my head with oil; my cup runneth over.

Commentary

In the face of seeming opposition and conflict, I shall succeed, for I will continue to outpicture the abundance that I am now conscious of being.

My head (consciousness) will continue to overflow with the joy of being God.

VII

Surely goodness and mercy shall follow me all the days of my life; and I will dwell in the house of the Lord forever.

Commentary
Because I am now conscious of being good and merciful, signs of goodness and mercy are compelled to follow me all the days of my life, for I will continue to dwell in the house (or consciousness) of being God (good) forever.

26

GETHSEMANE

Then cometh Jesus with them unto a place called Gethsemane, and saith unto the disciples, Sit ye here, while I go and pray yonder.

—MATTHEW 26:36

A most wonderful mystical romance is told in the story of Jesus in the Garden of Gethsemane, but man has failed to see the light of its symbology and has mistakenly interpreted this mystical union as an agonizing experience in which Jesus pleaded in vain with His Father to change His destiny.

Gethsemane is, to the mystic, the Garden of Creation—the place in consciousness where man goes to realize his defined objectives. Gethsemane is a compound word meaning to press out an oily substance: Geth, to press out, and Shemen, an oily substance.

The story of Gethsemane reveals to the mystic, in dramatic symbology, the act of creation.

Just as man contains within himself an oily substance which, in the act of creation, is pressed out into a likeness of himself, so he has within himself a divine principle (his consciousness) which conditions itself as a state of consciousness and without assistance presses out or objectifies itself.

A garden is a cultivated piece of ground, a specially prepared field, where seeds of the gardener's own choice are planted and cultivated.

Gethsemane is such a garden, the place in consciousness where the mystic goes with his properly defined objectives. This garden is entered when man takes his attention from the world round about him and places it on his objectives.

Man's clarified desires are seeds containing the power and plans of self-expression and, like the seeds within man, these, too, are buried within an oily substance (a joyful, thankful attitude of mind).

As man contemplates being and possessing that which he desires to be and to possess, he has begun the process of pressing out or the spiritual act of creation.

These seeds are pressed out and planted when man loses himself in a wild, mad state of joy, consciously feeling and claiming himself to be that which he formerly desired to be.

Desires expressed, or pressed out, result in the passing of that particular desire.

Man cannot possess a thing and still desire to possess it at one and the same time. So, as one consciously appropriates the feeling of being the thing desired, this desire to be the thing passes—is realized.

The receptive attitude of mind, feeling and receiving the impression of being the thing desired, is the fertile ground or womb which receives the seed (defined objective).

The seed which is pressed out of a man grows into the likeness of the man from whom it was pressed.

Likewise, the mystical seed, your conscious claim that you are that which you heretofore desired to be, will grow into the likeness of you from whom and into whom it is pressed.

Yes, Gethsemane is the cultivated garden of romance where the disciplined man goes to press seeds of joy (defined desires) out of himself into his receptive attitude of mind, there to care for and nurture them by consciously walking in the joy of being all that formerly he desired to be.

Feel with the Great Gardener the secret thrill of knowing that things and qualities not now seen will be seen as soon as these conscious impressions grow and ripen to maturity.

Your consciousness is Lord and Husband [Isa. 54:5]; the conscious state in which you dwell is wife or beloved. This state made visible is your son bearing witness of you, his father and mother, for your visible world is made in the image and likeness [Gen. 2:26] of the state of consciousness in which you live; your world and the fullness thereof are nothing more or less than your defined consciousness objectified.

Knowing this to be true, see to it that you choose well the mother of your children—that conscious state in which you live, your conception of yourself.

The wise man chooses his wife with great discretion. He realizes that his children must inherit the qualities of their parents and so he devotes much time and care to the selection of their mother. The mystic knows that the conscious state in which he lives is the choice that he has made of a wife, the mother of his children, that this state must in time embody itself within his world; so he is ever select in his choice and always claims himself to be his highest ideal.

He consciously defines himself as that which he desires to be.

When man realizes that the conscious state in which he lives is the choice that he has made of a mate, he will be more careful of his moods and feelings. He will not permit himself to react to suggestions of fear, lack or any undesirable impression. Such suggestions of lack could never pass the watch of the disciplined mind of the mystic, for he knows that every conscious claim must in time be expressed as a condition of his world—of his environment.

So, he remains faithful to his beloved, his defined objective, by defining and claiming and feeling himself to be that which he desires to express. Let a man ask himself if his defined objective would be a thing of joy and beauty if it were realized.

If his answer is in the affirmative, then he may know that his choice of a bride is a princess of Israel, a daughter of Judah, for every defined objective which expresses joy when realized is a daughter of Judah, the king of praise.

Jesus took with Him into His hour of prayer His disciples, or disciplined attributes of mind, and commanded them to watch while He prayed, so that no thought or belief that would deny the realization of His desire might enter His consciousness.

Follow the example of Jesus, who, with His desires clearly defined, entered the Garden of Gethsemane (the state of joy) accompanied by His disciples (His disciplined mind) to lose Himself in a wild joy of realization.

The fixing of His attention on His objective was His command to His disciplined mind to watch and remain faithful to that fixation. Contemplating the joy that would be His on realizing His desire, He began the spiritual act of generation, the act of pressing out the mystical seed—His defined desire.

In this fixation He remained, claiming and feeling Himself to be that which He (before He entered Gethsemane) desired to be, until His whole being (consciousness) was bathed in an oily sweat (joy) resembling blood (life), in short, until His whole consciousness was permeated with the living, sustained joy of being His defined objective.

As this fixation is accomplished so that the mystic knows by his feeling of joy that he has passed from his former conscious state into his present consciousness, the Passover or Crucifixion is attained.

This crucifixion or fixation of the new conscious claim is followed by the Sabbath, a time of rest. There is always an interval of time between the impression and its expression, between the conscious claim and its embodiment. This interval is called the Sabbath, the period of rest or non-effort (the day of entombment).

To walk unmoved in the consciousness of being or possessing a certain state is to keep the Sabbath.

The story of the crucifixion beautifully expresses this mystical stillness or rest. We are told that after Jesus cried out, "It is finished!" [John 19:30], He was placed in a tomb. There He remained for the entire Sabbath.

When the new state or consciousness is appropriated so you feel, by this appropriation, fixed and secure in the knowledge that it is finished, then you, too, will cry out, "It is finished!" and will enter the tomb or Sabbath, an interval of time in which you will walk unmoved in the conviction that your new consciousness must be resurrected (made visible).

Easter, the day of resurrection, falls on the first Sunday after the full moon in Aries. The mystical reason for this is simple. A defined area will not precipitate itself in the form of rain until this area reaches the point of saturation; just so the state in which you dwell will not express itself until the whole is permeated with the consciousness that it is so—it is finished.

Your defined objective is the imaginary state, just as the equator is the imaginary line across which the sun must pass to mark the beginning of spring. This state, like the moon, has no light or life of itself; but will reflect the light of consciousness or sun—"I am the light of the world" [Matt. 5:14; John 8:12; John 9:5; John 12:46]—"I am the resurrection and the life" [John 11:25].

As Easter is determined by the full moon in Aries, so, too, is the resurrection of your conscious claim determined by the full consciousness of your claim, by actually living as this new conception.

Most men fail to resurrect their objectives because they fail to remain faithful to their newly defined state until this fullness is attained.

If man would bear in mind the fact that there can be no Easter or day of resurrection until after the full moon, he would realize that the state into which he has consciously passed will be expressed or resurrected only after he has remained within the state of being his defined objective.

Until his whole self thrills with the feeling of actually being his conscious claim, in consciously living in this state of being it, and only in this way, will man ever resurrect or realize his desire.

] 27 [

A FORMULA FOR VICTORY

Every place that the sole of your foot shall tread upon, that have
I given unto you.

—JOSHUA 1:3

The majority of people are familiar with the story of
Joshua capturing the city of Jericho.

What they do not know is that this story is the perfect
formula for Victory, under any circumstances and against all
odds.

It is recorded that Joshua was armed only with the knowledge that every place that the sole of his foot should tread
upon would be given to him; that he desired to capture or
tread upon the city of Jericho but found the walls separating
him from the city impassable.

It seemed physically impossible for Joshua to get beyond
these massive walls and stand upon the city of Jericho. Yet, he
was *driven* by the knowledge of the promise that, regardless
of the barriers and obstacles separating him from his desires,
if he could but stand upon the city, it would be given to him.

The Book of Joshua further records that instead of fighting this giant problem of the wall, Joshua employed the services of the harlot, Rahab, and sent her as a spy into the city. As Rahab entered her house, which stood in the midst of the city, Joshua—who was securely barred by the impassable walls of Jericho—blew on his trumpet seven times. At the seventh blast, the walls crumbled and Joshua entered the city victoriously.

To the uninitiated, this story is senseless.

To the one who sees it as a psychological drama, rather than as a historical record, it is most revealing.

If we would follow the example of Joshua, our victory would be similarly simple.

Joshua symbolizes to you, the reader, your present state; the city of Jericho symbolizes your desire, or defined objective.

The walls of Jericho symbolize the obstacles between you and the realization of your objectives. The foot symbolizes the understanding; placing the sole of the foot upon a definite place indicates fixing a definite psychological state.

Rahab, the spy, is your ability to travel secretly or psychologically to any place in space. Consciousness knows no frontier. No one can stop you from dwelling psychologically at any point, or in any state in time or space.

Regardless of the physical barriers separating you from your objective, you can, without effort or help of anyone, annihilate time, space and barriers.

Thus, you can dwell, psychologically, in the desired state. So, although you may not be able to tread physically upon a state or city, you can always tread *psychologically* upon any desired state. By treading psychologically, I mean that you can now, this moment, close your eyes and after visualizing or imagining a place or state other than your present one, actually FEEL that you are now in such a place or state. You can feel this condition to be so real that upon opening your eyes you are amazed to find that you are not physically there.

A harlot, as you know, gives to all men that which they ask of her. Rahab, the harlot, symbolizes your infinite capacity to psychologically assume any desirable state without questioning whether or not you are physically or morally fit to do so.

You can today capture the modern city of Jericho or your defined objective if you will psychologically re-enact this story of Joshua; but to capture the city and realize your desires, you must carefully follow the formula of victory as laid down in this book of Joshua.

This is the application of this victorious formula as a modern mystic reveals it today:

First: define your objective (not the manner of obtaining it)—but your objective, pure and simple; know exactly what it is you desire so that you have a clear mental picture of it.

Secondly: take your attention away from the obstacles which separate you from your objective and place your thought on the objective itself.

Thirdly: close your eyes and FEEL that you are already in the city or state that you would capture. Remain within this psychological state until you get a conscious reaction of complete satisfaction in this victory. Then, by simply opening your eyes, return to your former conscious state.

This secret journey into the desired state, with its subsequent psychological reaction of complete satisfaction, is all that is necessary to bring about total victory.

This victorious psychical state will embody itself despite all opposition. It has the plan and power of self-expression.

From this point forward, follow the example of Joshua, who, after psychologically dwelling in the desired state until he received a complete conscious reaction of victory, did nothing more to bring about this victory than to blow seven times on his trumpet.

The seventh blast symbolizes the seventh day, a time of stillness or rest, the interval between the subjective and objective states, a period of pregnancy or joyful expectancy.

This stillness is not the stillness of the body but rather the stillness of the mind—a perfect passivity, which is not indolence but a living stillness born of trust in this immutable law of consciousness.

Those not familiar with this law or formula for victory, in attempting to still their minds, succeed only in acquiring a quiet tension, which is nothing more than compressed anxiety.

But you, who know this law, will find that after capturing the psychological state which would be yours if you were already victoriously and actually entrenched in that city, will move forward towards the physical realization of your desires.

You will do this without doubt or fear, in a state of mind fixed in the knowledge of a prearranged victory.

You will not be afraid of the enemy, because the outcome has been determined by the psychological state that preceded the physical offensive; and all the forces of heaven and earth cannot stop the victorious fulfillment of that state.

Stand still in the psychological state defined as your objective until you feel the thrill of Victory.

Then, with confidence born of the knowledge of this law, watch the physical realization of your objective.

> . . . *Set your self, stand still and watch the salvation of the Law with you . . .*

AWAKENED
IMAGINATION

AWAKENED IMAGINATION

by

Neville

1954

1946

The Power which makes the achievement of aims . . . the attainment of desires . . . inevitable.

Imagination, the real and eternal world of which this Vegetable Universe is but a faint shadow. What is the life of Man but Art and Science?

—William Blake, *Jerusalem*

Imagination is more important than knowledge.

—Albert Einstein, *On Science*

To Bill

CONTENTS

1

WHO IS YOUR IMAGINATION?

I rest not from my great task

    To open the Eternal Worlds, to open the immortal Eyes Of
Man inwards into the Worlds of Thought: into Eternity Ever
expanding in the Bosom of God, the Human Imagination.

                            —BLAKE, *JERUSALEM* 5:18–20

Certain words in the course of long use gather so many
strange connotations that they almost cease to mean
anything at all. Such a word is *imagination*. This word is made
to serve all manner of ideas, some of them directly opposed to
one another. *Fancy, thought, hallucination, suspicion:* indeed, so
wide is its use and so varied its meanings, the word *imagination* has no status nor fixed significance.

For example, we ask a man to "use his imagination", meaning that his present outlook is too restricted and therefore
not equal to the task. In the next breath, we tell him that his
ideas are "pure imagination", thereby implying that his ideas
are unsound. We speak of a jealous or suspicious person as a
"victim of his own imagination", meaning that his thoughts

are untrue. A minute later we pay a man the highest tribute by describing him as a "man of imagination".

Thus the word *imagination* has no definite meaning. Even the dictionary gives us no help. It defines imagination as (1) the picturing power or act of the mind, the constructive or creative principle; (2) a phantasm; (3) an irrational notion or belief; (4) planning, plotting or scheming as involving mental construction.

I identify the central figure of the Gospels with human imagination, the power which makes the forgiveness of sins, the achievement of our goals, inevitable.

All things were made by Him; and without Him was not anything made that was made. [John 1:3]

There is only one thing in the world, Imagination, and all our deformations of it.

He is despised and rejected of men; a man of sorrows, and acquainted with grief. [Isaiah 53:3]

Imagination is the very gateway of reality.

"Man", said Blake, "is either the ark of God or a phantom of the earth and of the water". "Naturally he is only a natural organ subject to Sense". "The Eternal Body of Man is The Imagination: that is God himself, The Divine Body. יש״ *[yod, shin, ayin; from right to the left]:* Jesus: we are His Members".

I know of no greater and truer definition of the Imagination than that of Blake. By imagination we have the power to be anything we desire to be.

Through imagination, we disarm and transform the violence of the world. Our most intimate as well as our most casual relationships become imaginative, as we awaken to *"the mystery hid from the ages"* [Col. 1:26], that Christ in us is our imagination.

We then realize that only as we live by imagination can we truly be said to live at all.

I want this book to be the simplest, clearest, frankest work I have the power to make it, that I may encourage you to function imaginatively, that you may open your "Immortal Eyes inwards into the Worlds of Thought" [William Blake], where you behold every desire of your heart as ripe grain "white already to harvest" [John 4:35].

I am come that they might have life, and that they might have it more abundantly. [John 10:10]

> *The abundant life that Christ promised us is ours to experience* now, *but not until we have the sense of Christ* as our imagination *can we experience it.*

The mystery hid from the ages . . . *Christ in you, the hope of glory* [Col. 1:26, 27], is your imagination.

This is the mystery which I am ever striving to realize more keenly myself and to urge upon others.

Imagination is our redeemer, "the Lord from Heaven" born of man but not begotten of man [The Nicene-Constantinopolitan Creed or the Symbol of Faith, 325/381 A.D.].

Every man is Mary and birth to Christ must give.

If the story of the immaculate conception[1] and birth of Christ appears irrational to man, it is only because it is misread as biography, history, and cosmology, and the modern explorers of the imagination do not help by calling It the unconscious or subconscious mind.

---

1 Neville uses this term in reference to what is traditionally called the Virgin Birth.

Imagination's birth and growth is the gradual transition from a God of tradition to a God of experience. If the birth of Christ in man seems slow, it is only because man is unwilling to let go the comfortable but false anchorage of tradition.

When imagination is discovered as the first principle of religion, the stone of literal understanding will have felt the rod of Moses and, like the rock of Zion [Isa. 28:16; Rom. 9:33], issue forth the water of psychological meaning to quench the thirst of humanity; and all who take the proffered cup and live a life according to this truth will transform the water of psychological meaning into the wine of forgiveness. Then, like the good Samaritan [Luke 10:33–35], they will pour it on the wounds of all.

The Son of God is not to be found in history, nor in any external form. He can only be found as the imagination of him in whom His presence becomes manifest.

O, would thy heart but be a manger for His birth! God would once more become a child on earth. [Angelus Silesius, a 17th century poet]

Man is the garden in which this only-begotten Son of God sleeps. He awakens this Son by lifting his imagination up to heaven and clothing men in godlike stature. We must go on imagining better than the best we know.

Man in the moment of his awakening to the imaginative life must meet the test of Sonship.

"Father, reveal Thy Son in me" [James Montgomery] and

"It pleased God to reveal His Son in me". [Gal. 1:15, 16]

The supreme test of Sonship is the forgiveness of sin. The test that your imagination is Christ Jesus, the Son of God, is your ability to forgive sin. Sin means *missing one's mark in life, falling short of one's ideal, failing to achieve one's aim.* Forgiveness means identification of man with his ideal or aim in life. This is the work of awakened imagination, the supreme work, for it tests man's ability to enter into and partake of the nature of his opposite.

Let the weak man say, I am strong. [Joel 3:10]

Reasonably, this is impossible. Only awakened imagination can enter into and partake of the nature of its opposite.

This conception of Christ Jesus as human imagination raises these fundamental questions: Is imagination a power sufficient, not merely to enable me to assume that I am strong, but is it also of itself capable of executing the idea?

Suppose that I desire to be in some other place or situation. Could I, by imagining myself into such a state and place, bring about their physical realization? Suppose I could not afford the journey and suppose my present social and financial status oppose the idea that I want to realize. Would imagination be sufficient of itself to incarnate these desires? Does imagination comprehend reason? By reason, I mean deductions from the observations of the senses.

Does it recognize the external world of facts? In the practical way of everyday life is imagination a complete guide to behaviour?

Suppose I am capable of acting with continuous imagination, that is, suppose I am capable of sustaining the feeling of my wish fulfilled, will my assumption harden into fact?

And, if it does harden into fact, shall I on reflection find that my actions through the period of incubation have been reasonable? Is my imagination a power sufficient, not merely to assume the feeling of the wish fulfilled, but is it also of itself capable of incarnating the idea?

After assuming that I am already what I want to be, must I continually guide myself by reasonable ideas and actions in order to bring about the fulfillment of my assumption?

Experience has convinced me that an assumption, though false, if persisted in, will harden into fact, that continuous imagination is sufficient for all things, and all my reasonable plans and actions will never make up for my lack of continuous imagination.

Is it not true that the teachings of the Gospels can only be received in terms of faith and that the Son of God is constantly looking for signs of faith in people—that is, faith in their own imagination?

Is not the promise

Believe that ye receive and ye shall receive [Mark 11:24],

the same as "Imagine that you are and you shall be"? Was it not an imaginary state in which Moses *"Endured, as seeing Him who is invisible"* [Heb. 11:27]?

Was it not by the power of his own imagination that he endured?

Truth depends upon the intensity of the imagination, not upon external facts. Facts are the fruit bearing witness of the use or misuse of the imagination.

Man becomes what he imagines. He has a self-determined history. Imagination is the way, the truth, the life revealed.

We cannot get hold of truth with the logical mind. Where the natural man of sense sees a bud, imagination sees a rose full-blown.

Truth cannot be encompassed by facts.

As we awaken to the imaginative life, we discover that to imagine a thing is to make it so, that a true judgment need not conform to the external reality to which it relates.

The imaginative man does not deny the reality of the sensuous outer world of Becoming, but he knows that it is the inner world of continuous Imagination that is the force by which the sensuous outer world of Becoming is brought to pass. He sees the outer world and all its happenings as projections of the inner world of Imagination.

To him, everything is a manifestation of the mental activity which goes on in man's imagination, without the sensuous reasonable man being aware of it.

But he realizes that every man must become conscious of this inner activity and see the relationship between the inner causal world of imagination and the sensuous outer world of effects.

It is a marvelous thing to find that you can imagine yourself into the state of your fulfilled desire and escape from the jails which ignorance built.

The Real Man is a Magnificent Imagination. It is this *self* that must be awakened.

Awake thou that steepest, and arise from the dead, and Christ shall give thee light. [Eph. 5:14]

The moment man discovers that his imagination is Christ, he accomplishes acts which on this level can only be called miraculous. But until man has the sense of Christ *as his imagination,*

"You did not choose me, I have chosen you" [John 15:16]

he will see everything in pure objectivity without any subjective relationship.

Not realizing that all that he encounters is part of himself, he rebels at the thought that he has chosen the conditions of his life, that they are related by affinity to his own mental activity.

Man must firmly come to believe that reality lies within him and not without.

Although others have bodies, a life of their own, their reality is rooted in you, ends in you, as yours ends in God.

2

SEALED INSTRUCTIONS

The first power that meets us at the threshold of the soul's domain is the power of imagination.

—Dr. Franz Hartmann

I was first made conscious of the power, nature, and redemptive function of imagination through the teachings of my friend Abdullah: and through subsequent experiences, I learned that Jesus was a symbol of the coming of imagination to man, that the test of His birth in man was the individual's ability to forgive sin; that is, his ability to identify himself or another with his aim in life.

Without the identification of man with his aim, the forgiveness of sin is an impossibility, and only the Son of God can forgive sin.

Therefore, man's ability to identify himself with his aim, though reason and his senses deny it, is proof of the birth of Christ in him.

To passively surrender to appearances and bow before the

evidence of facts is to confess that Christ is not yet born in you.

Although this teaching shocked and repelled me at first—for I was a convinced and earnest Christian, and did not then know that Christianity could not be inherited by the mere accident of birth but must be consciously adopted as a way of life—it stole later on, through visions, mystical revelations, and practical experiences, into my understanding and found its interpretation in a deeper mood. But I must confess that it is a trying time when those things are shaken which one has always taken for granted.

Seest thou these great buildings? There shall not be left one stone upon another that shall not be thrown down. [Mark 13:2]

Not one stone of literal understanding will be left after one drinks the water of psychological meaning.

All that has been built up by natural religion is cast into the flames of mental fire. Yet, what better way is there to understand Christ Jesus than to identify the central character of the Gospels with human imagination—knowing that, every time you exercise your imagination lovingly on behalf of another, you are literally mediating God to man and thereby feeding and clothing Christ Jesus and that, whenever you imagine evil against another, you are literally beating and crucifying Christ Jesus?

Every imagination of man is either the cup of cold water or the sponge of vinegar to the parched lips of Christ.

Let none of you imagine evil in your hearts against his neighbor, warned the prophet Zechariah [8:17].

When man heeds this advice, he will awake from the imposed sleep of Adam into the full consciousness of the Son of God. *He is in the world, and the world is made by Him, and the world knows Him not* [approx.; John 1:10]: Human Imagination.

I asked myself many times, "If my imagination is Christ Jesus and all things are possible to Christ Jesus, are all things possible to me?"

Through experience, I have come to know that, when I identify myself with my aim in life, then Christ is awake in me.

Christ is sufficient for all things. *["For in Him dwelleth all the fullness of the Godhead bodily, And ye are complete in Him, which is the head of all principality and power"* (Col. 2:9, 10); *"My grace is sufficient for thee"* (2 Cor. 12:9).]

I lay down My life that I might take it again. No man taketh it from Me, but I lay it down of Myself. [John 10:17, 18]

What a comfort it is to know that all that I experience is the result of my own standard of beliefs; that I am the center of my own web of circumstances and that as I change, so must my outer world!

The world presents different appearances according as our states of consciousness differ.

What we see when we are identified with a state cannot be seen when we are no longer fused with it.

By *state* is meant all that man believes and consents to as true.

No idea presented to the mind can realize itself unless the mind accepts it.

It depends on the acceptance, the state with which we are identified, how things present themselves. In the fusion of imagination and states is to be found the shaping of the world as it seems. The world is a revelation of the states with which imagination is fused. It is the state *from* which we think that determines the objective world in which we live. The rich man, the poor man, the good man, the thief are what they are by virtue of the states *from* which they view the world. On the distinction between these states depends the distinction between the worlds of these men. Individually so different is this same world. It is not the actions and behaviour of the good man that should be matched but his point of view.

Outer reforms are useless if the inner state is not changed.

Success is gained not by imitating the outer actions of the successful but by right inner actions and inner talking.

If we detach ourselves from a state, and we may at any moment, the conditions and circumstances to which that union gave being vanish.

It was in the fall of 1933 in New York City that I approached Abdullah with a problem. He asked me one simple question, "What do you want?"

I told him that I would like to spend the winter in Barbados, but that I was broke. I literally did not have a nickel.

"If you will imagine yourself to be *in* Barbados", said he, "thinking and viewing the world *from* that state of consciousness instead of thinking *of* Barbados, you will spend the winter there.

"You must not concern yourself with the ways and means of getting there, for the state of consciousness of already being in Barbados, if occupied by your imagination, will devise the means best suited to realize itself."

Man lives by committing himself to invisible states, by fusing his imagination with what he knows to be other than himself, and in this union he experiences the results of that fusion. No one can lose what he has, save by detachment from the state where the things experienced have their natural life.

"You must imagine yourself right into the state of your fulfilled desire". Abdullah told me, "and fall asleep viewing the world from Barbados."

The world which we describe from observation must be as we describe it relative to ourselves.

Our imagination connects us with the state desired.

But we must use imagination masterfully, not as an on-looker thinking *of* the end, but as a partaker *thinking from* the end.

We must actually *be* there in imagination.

If we do this, our subjective experience will be realized objectively.

"This is not mere fancy", said he, "but a truth you can prove by experience."

His appeal to enter *into* the wish fulfilled was the secret of thinking *from* the end. Every state is already there as "mere possibility" as long as you think *of* it, but is overpoweringly real when you think *from* it. Thinking from the end is the way of Christ.

I began right there and then, fixing my thoughts beyond the limits of sense, beyond that aspect to which my present state gave being, towards the feeling of already being *in* Barbados and viewing the world *from* that standpoint.

He emphasized the importance of the state *from* which man views the world as he falls asleep. All prophets claim that the voice of God is chiefly heard by man in dreams.

In a dream, in a vision of the night, when deep sleep falleth upon men, in slumbering upon the bed: then he openeth the ears of men, and sealeth their instruction. [Job 33:15, 16]

That night and for several nights thereafter, I fell asleep in the assumption that I was in my father's house in Barbados. Within a month, I received a letter from my brother, saying that he had a strong desire to have the family together at Christmas and asking me to use the enclosed steamship ticket for Barbados. I sailed two days after I received my brother's letter and spent a wonderful winter in Barbados.

This experience has convinced me that man can be anything he pleases if he will make the conception habitual and think *from* the end.

It has also shown me that I can no longer excuse myself by placing the blame on the world of external things—that my good and my evil have no dependency except from myself—that it depends on the state *from* which I view the world how things present themselves.

Man, who is free in his choice, acts from conceptions which he freely, though not always wisely, chooses. All conceivable states are awaiting our choice and occupancy, but no amount of rationalizing will of itself yield us the state of consciousness which is the only thing worth having.

The imaginative image is the only thing to seek.

The ultimate purpose of imagination is to create in us "the spirit of Jesus", which is continual forgiveness of sin, continual identification of man with his ideal.

Only by identifying ourselves with our aim can we forgive ourselves for having missed it. All else is labor in vain. On this path, to whatever place or state we convey our imagination, to that place or state we will gravitate physically also.

In My Father's house are many mansions; if it were not so, I would have told you. I go to prepare a place for you. And if I go and prepare a place for you, I will come again, and receive you unto Myself: that where I am, there ye may be also. [John 14:2, 3]

By sleeping in my father's house in my imagination as though I slept there in the flesh, I fused my imagination with that state and was compelled to experience that state in the flesh also.

So vivid was this state to me, I could have been seen in my father's house had any sensitive entered the room where in imagination I was sleeping. A man can be seen where in imagination he is, for a man must be where his imagination is, for his imagination is himself. This I know from experience, for I have been seen by a few to whom I desired to be seen, when physically I was hundreds of miles away.

I, by the intensity of my imagination and feeling, imagining and feeling myself to be *in* Barbados instead of merely thinking *of* Barbados, had spanned the vast Atlantic to influence my brother into desiring my presence to complete the family circle at Christmas.

Thinking from the end, from the feeling of my wish fulfilled, was the source of everything that happened as outer cause, such as my brother's impulse to send me a steamship ticket; and it was also the cause of everything that appeared as results.

In *Ideas of Good and Evil*, W. B. Yeats, having described a few experiences similar to this experience of mine, writes:

> *If all who have described events like this have not dreamed,*
> *we should rewrite our histories, for all men, certainly*
> *all imaginative men, must be forever casting forth*
> *enchantments, glamour, illusions; and all men, especially*
> *tranquil men who have no powerful egotistic life, must be*
> *continually passing under their power.*

Determined imagination, thinking from the end, is the beginning of all miracles.

I would like to give you an immense belief in miracles, but a miracle is only the name given by those who have no knowledge of the power and function of imagination to the works of imagination.

Imagining oneself into the feeling of the wish fulfilled is the means by which a new state is entered. This gives the state the quality of is-ness.

Hermes tells us:

That which *is*, is manifested; that which has been or shall be, is unmanifested, but not dead; for Soul, the eternal activity of God, animates all things.

The future must become the present in the imagination of the one who would wisely and consciously create circumstances.

We must translate vision into Being, thinking *of* into thinking *from*. Imagination must center itself in some state and view the world *from* that state. Thinking *from* the end is an intense perception of the world of fulfilled desire.

Thinking *from* the state desired is creative living. Ignorance of this ability to think *from* the end is bondage.

It is the root of all bondage with which man is bound. To passively surrender to the evidence of the senses underestimates the capacities of the Inner Self.

Once man accepts thinking *from* the end as a creative principle in which he can cooperate, then he is redeemed from the absurdity of ever attempting to achieve his objective by merely thinking *of* it.

Construct all ends according to the pattern of fulfilled desire.

The whole of life is just the appeasement of hunger, and the infinite states of consciousness from which a man can view the world are purely a means of satisfying that hunger.

The principle upon which each state is organized is some form of hunger to lift the passion for self-gratification to ever higher and higher levels of experience.

Desire is the mainspring of the mental machinery. It is a blessed thing. It is a right and natural craving which has a state of consciousness as its right and natural satisfaction.

But one thing I do, forgetting the things which are behind, and stretching forward to the things which are before, I press on toward the goal. [Phil. 3:13, 14]

It is necessary to have an aim in life. Without an aim, we drift. "What wantest thou of Me?" *[What wilt thou that I shall do unto thee? (Luke 18:41)]* is the implied question asked most often by the central figure of the Gospels. In defining your aim, you must want it.

As the hart panteth after the water brooks, so panteth my soul after Thee, O, God. [Ps. 42:1]

It is lack of this passionate direction to life that makes man fail of accomplishment.

The spanning of the bridge between desire—thinking of— and satisfaction—thinking from—is all-important.

We must move mentally from thinking *of* the end to thinking *from* the end.

This, reason could never do. By its nature, it is restricted to the evidence of the senses; but imagination, having no such limitation, can.

Desire exists to be gratified in the activity of imagination.

Through imagination, man escapes from the limitation of the senses and the bondage of reason.

There is no stopping the man who can think *from* the end. Nothing can stop him. He creates the means and grows his way out of limitation into ever greater and greater mansions of the Lord.

It does not matter what he has been or what he is. All that matters is "what does he want?"

He knows that the world is a manifestation of the mental activity which goes on within himself, so he strives to determine and control the ends *from* which he thinks.

In his imagination he dwells in the end, confident that he shall dwell there in the flesh also.

He puts his whole trust in the feeling of the wish fulfilled and lives by committing himself to that state, for the art of fortune is to tempt him so to do.

Like the man at the pool of Bethesda, he is ready for the moving of the waters of imagination.

Knowing that every desire is ripe grain to him who knows how to think *from* the end, he is indifferent to mere reasonable probability and confident that through continuous imagination his assumptions will harden into fact.

But how to persuade men everywhere that thinking *from* the end is the only living, how to foster it in every activity of man, how to reveal it as the plenitude of life and not the compensation of the disappointed: that is the problem.

Life is a controllable thing.

You can experience what you please once you realize that you are His Son, and that you are what you are by virtue of the state of consciousness *from* which you think and view the world,

Son, Thou art ever with Me, and all that I have is Thine.
[Luke 15:31]

] **3** [

HIGHWAYS OF THE INNER WORLD

And the children struggled within her . . . and the Lord said unto her, two nations are in thy womb, and two manner of people shall be separated from thy bowels; and the one people shall be stronger than the other people; and the elder shall serve the younger.

—Genesis 25:22, 23

Duality is an inherent condition of life. Everything that exists is double. Man is a dual creature with contrary principles embedded in his nature. They war within him and present attitudes to life which are antagonistic. This conflict is the eternal enterprise, the war in heaven, the never-ending struggle of the younger or inner man of imagination to assert His supremacy over the elder or outer man of sense.

The first shall be last and the last shall be first. [Matt. 19:30] *He it is, Who coming after me is preferred before me.* [John 1:27] *The second Man is the Lord from heaven.* [1 Cor. 15:47]

Man begins to awake to the imaginative life the moment he feels the presence of another being in himself.

In your limbs lie nations twain, rival races from their birth; one the mastery shall gain, the younger o'er the elder reign.

There are two distinct centers of thought or outlooks on the world possessed by every man.

The Bible speaks of these two outlooks as natural and spiritual.

The natural man receiveth not the things of the Spirit of God: for they are foolishness unto him: neither can he know them, because they are spiritually discerned. [1 Cor. 2:14]

Man's inner body is as real in the world of subjective experience as his outer physical body is real in the world of external realities, but the inner body expresses a more fundamental part of reality.

This existing inner body of man must be consciously exercised and directed.

The inner world of thought and feeling to which the inner body is attuned has its real structure and exists in its own higher space.

There are two kinds of movement, one that is according to the inner body and another that is according to the outer body. The movement which is according to the inner body is causal, but the outer movement is under compulsion. The inner movement determines the outer which is joined to it, bringing into the outer a movement that is similar to the actions of the inner body. Inner movement is the force by which all events are brought to pass. Outer movement is subject to the compulsion applied to it by the movement of the inner body.

Whenever the actions of the inner body match the actions which the outer must take to appease desire, that desire will be realized.

Construct mentally a drama which implies that your desire

is realized and make it one which involves movement of self. Immobilize your outer physical self. Act precisely as though you were going to take a nap, and start the predetermined action in imagination.

A vivid representation of the action is the beginning of that action. Then, as you are falling asleep, consciously imagine yourself into the scene. The length of the sleep is not important, a short nap is sufficient, but carrying the action into sleep thickens fancy into fact.

At first your thoughts may be like rambling sheep that have no shepherd. Don't despair. Should your attention stray seventy times seven, bring it back seventy times seven to its predetermined course until from sheer exhaustion it follows the appointed path. The inner journey must never be without direction. When you take to the inner road, it is to do what you did mentally before you started. You go for the prize you have already seen and accepted.

In *The Road to Xanadu*, Professor John Livingston Lowes says:

> But I have long had the feeling, which this study had matured to a conviction, that Fancy and Imagination are not two powers at all, but one. The valid distinction which exists between them lies, not in the materials with which they operate, but in the degree of intensity of the operant power itself. Working at high tension, the imaginative energy assimilates and transmutes; keyed low, the same energy aggregates and yokes together those images which at its highest pitch, it merges indissolubly into one.

Fancy assembles, imagination fuses.

Here is a practical application of this theory. A year ago, a blind girl living in the city of San Francisco found herself confronted with a transportation problem. A rerouting of buses forced her to make three transfers between her home and her office. This lengthened her trip from fifteen minutes to two hours and fifteen minutes. She thought seriously about this problem and came to the decision that a car was the solution. She knew that she could not drive a car but felt that she could be driven in one. Putting this theory to the test that "whenever the actions of the inner self correspond to the actions which the outer, physical self must take to appease desire, that desire will be realized", she said to herself. "I will sit here and imagine that I am being driven to my office."

Sitting in her living room, she began to imagine herself seated in a car. She felt the rhythm of the motor. She imagined that she smelled the odor of gasoline, felt the motion of the car, touched the sleeve of the driver and felt that the driver was a man. She felt the car stop, and turning to her companion, said, "Thank you very much, sir."

To which he replied, "The pleasure is all mine."

Then she stepped from the car and heard the door snap shut as she closed it.

She told me that she centered her imagination on being *in* a car and, although blind, viewed the city *from* her imaginary ride. She did not think *of* the ride. She thought *from* the ride and all that it implied. This controlled and subjectively directed purposive ride raised her imagination to its full potency. She kept her purpose ever before her, knowing there was cohesion in purposive inner movement. In these mental journeys an emotional continuity must be sustained—the emotion of fulfilled desire. Expectancy and desire were so intensely joined that they passed at once from a mental state into a physical act.

The inner self moves along the predetermined course best when the emotions collaborate. The inner self must be fired, and it is best fired by the thought of great deeds and personal gain. We must take pleasure in our actions.

On two successive days, the blind girl took her imaginary ride, giving it all the joy and sensory vividness of reality. A few hours after her second imaginary ride, a friend told her of a story in the evening paper. It was a story of a man who was interested in the blind. The blind girl phoned him and stated her problem. The very next day, on his way home, he stopped in at a bar and while there had the urge to tell the story of the blind girl to his friend the proprietor. A total stranger, on hearing the story, volunteered to drive the blind girl home every day. The man who told the story then said, "If you will take her home, I will take her to work."

This was over a year ago, and since that day, this blind girl has been driven to and from her office by these two gentlemen. Now, instead of spending two hours and fifteen minutes on three buses, she is at her office in less than fifteen minutes. And on that first ride to her office, she turned to her good Samaritan and said, "Thank you very much, sir"; and he replied, "The pleasure is all mine."

Thus, the objects of her imagination were to her the realities of which the physical manifestation was only the witness.

The determinative animating principle was the imaginative ride. Her triumph could be a surprise only to those who did not know of her inner ride. She mentally viewed the world from this imaginative ride with such a clearness of vision that every aspect of the city attained identity.

These inner movements not only produce corresponding outer movements: this is the law which operates beneath all physical appearances.

He who practices these exercises of bilocation will develop unusual powers of concentration and quiescence and will inevitably achieve waking consciousness on the inner and dimensionally larger world.

Actualizing strongly, she fulfilled her desire, for, viewing the city *from* the feeling of her wish fulfilled, she matched the state desired and granted that to herself which sleeping men ask of God.

To realize your desire, an action must start in your imagination, apart from the evidence of the senses, involving movement of self and implying fulfillment of your desire. Whenever it is the action which the outer self takes to appease desire, that desire will be realized.

The movement of every visible object is caused not by things outside the body, but by things within it, which operate from within outward.

The journey is in yourself. You travel along the highways of the inner world. Without inner movement, it is impossible to bring forth anything. Inner action is introverted sensation. If you will construct mentally a drama which implies that you have realized your objective, then close your eyes and drop your thoughts inward, centering your imagination all the while in the predetermined action and partake in that action, you will become a self-determined being.

Inner action orders all things according to the nature of itself.

Try it and see whether a desirable ideal once formulated is possible, for only by this process of experiment can you realize your potentialities.

It is thus that this creative principle is being realized. So the clue to purposive living is to center your imagination in the action and feeling of fulfilled desire with such awareness, such sensitiveness, that you initiate and experience movement upon the inner world.

Ideas only act if they are felt, if they awaken inner movement. Inner movement is conditioned by self-motivation, outer movement by compulsion.

Wherever the sole of your foot shall tread, the same give I unto you.

and remember,

The Lord thy God in the midst of thee is mighty.

Zephaniah 3:17

Joshua 1:3

THE PRUNING SHEARS OF REVISION

The second Man is the Lord from Heaven.
—1 CORINTHIANS 15:47

Never will he say caterpillars. He'll say, "There's a lot of butterflies-as-is-to-be on our cabbages. Pure."

He won't say, "It's winter."

He'll say, "Summer's sleeping."

And there's no bud little enough nor sad-coloured enough for Kester not to callen it the beginnings of the blow.
—MARY WEBB, PRECIOUS BANE

The very first act of correction or cure is always "revise". One must start with oneself. It is one's attitude that must be changed.

What we are, that only can we see. [Emerson]

It is a most healthy and productive exercise to daily relive the day as you wish you had lived it, revising the scenes to make them conform to your ideals.

For instance, suppose today's mail brought disappointing

news. Revise the letter. Mentally rewrite it and make it conform to the news you wish you had received. Then, in imagination, read the revised letter over and over again. This is the essence of revision, and revision results in repeal.

The one requisite is to arouse your attention in a way and to such intensity that you become wholly absorbed in the revised action. You will experience an expansion and refinement of the senses by this imaginative exercise and eventually achieve vision.

But always remember that the ultimate purpose of this exercise is to create in you "the Spirit of Jesus", which is continual forgiveness of sin.

Revision is of greatest importance when the motive is to change oneself, when there is a sincere desire to be something different, when the longing is to awaken the ideal active spirit of forgiveness.

Without imagination, man remains a being of sin.

Man either goes forward to imagination or remains imprisoned in his senses. To go forward to imagination is to forgive. Forgiveness is the life of the imagination. The art of living is the art of forgiving.

Forgiveness is, in fact, experiencing in imagination the revised version of the day, experiencing in imagination what you wish you had experienced in the flesh.

Every time one really forgives—that is, every time one relives the event as it should have been lived—one is born again.

"Father, forgive them" is not the plea that comes once a year but the opportunity that comes every day. The idea of forgiving is a daily possibility, and, if it is sincerely done, it will lift man to higher and higher levels of being. He will experience a daily Easter, and Easter is the idea of rising transformed.

And that should be almost a continuous process.

Freedom and forgiveness are indissolubly linked.

Not to forgive is to be at war with ourselves, for we are freed according to our capacity to forgive.

Forgive, and you shall be forgiven. [Luke 6:37]

Forgive, not merely from a sense of duty or service; forgive because you want to.

Thy ways are ways of pleasantness and all thy paths are peace. [Prov. 3:17]

You must take pleasure in revision. You can forgive others effectively only when you have a sincere desire to identify them with their ideal. Duty has no momentum.

Forgiveness is a matter of deliberately withdrawing attention from the unrevised day and giving it full strength, and joyously, to the revised day. If a man begins to revise even a little of the vexations and troubles of the day, then he begins to work practically on himself. Every revision is a victory over himself and therefore a victory over his enemy.

A man's foes are those of his own household [Matt. 10:36] and his household is his state of mind. He changes his future as he revises his day.

When a man practices the art of forgiveness, of revision, however factual the scene on which sight then rests, he revises it with his imagination and gazes on one never before witnessed. The magnitude of the change which any act of revision involves makes such change appear wholly improbable to the realist—the unimaginative man; but the radical changes in the fortunes of the Prodigal [Luke 15:11–32] were all produced by a "change of heart".

The battle man fights is fought out *in his own imagination*. The man who does not revise the day has lost the vision of that life, into the likeness of which it is the true labour of the "Spirit of Jesus" to transform this life.

All things whatsoever ye would that men should do to you, even so do ye to them: for this is the law. [Matt. 7:12]

Here is the way an artist friend forgave herself and was set free from pain, annoyance and unfriendliness. Knowing that nothing but forgetfulness and forgiveness will bring us to new values, she cast herself upon her imagination and escaped from the prison of her senses. She writes:

"Thursday, I taught all day in the art school. Only one small thing marred the day. Coming into my afternoon classroom, I discovered the janitor had left all the chairs on top of the desks after cleaning the floor. As I lifted a chair down, it slipped from my grasp and struck me a sharp blow on the instep of my right foot. I immediately examined my thoughts and found that I had criticized the man for not doing his job properly. Since he had lost his helper, I realized he probably felt he had done more than enough and it was an unwanted gift that had bounced and hit me on the foot. Looking down at my foot, I saw both my skin and nylons were intact, so forgot the whole thing.

"That night, after I had been working intensely for about three hours on a drawing, I decided to make myself a cup of coffee. To my utter amazement, I couldn't manage my right foot at all and it was giving out great bumps of pain. I hopped over to a chair and took off my slipper to look at it. The entire foot was a strange purplish pink, swollen out of shape and red hot. I tried walking on it and found that it just flapped. I had no control over it whatsoever. It looked like one of two things:

either I had cracked a bone when I dropped the chair on it or something could be dislocated.

"No use speculating what it is. Better get rid of it right away.

"So I became quiet, all ready to melt myself into light. To my complete bewilderment, my imagination refused to cooperate. It just said 'No.'

"This sort of thing often happens when I am painting. I just started to argue 'Why not?' It just kept saying 'No.'

"Finally, I gave up and said, 'You know I am in pain. I am trying hard not to be frightened, but you are the boss. What do you want to do?'

"The answer: 'Go to bed and review the day's events.'

"So I said 'All right. But let me tell you if my foot isn't perfect by tomorrow morning, you have only yourself to blame.'

"After arranging the bed clothes so they didn't touch my foot, I started to review the day. It was slow going as I had difficulty keeping my attention away from my foot. I went through the whole day, saw nothing to add to the chair incident. But when I reached the early evening, I found myself coming face to face with a man who for the past year has made a point of not speaking. The first time this happened, I thought he had grown deaf. I had known him since school days, but we had never done more than say 'hello' and comment on the weather. Mutual friends assured me I had done nothing, that he had said he never liked me and finally decided it was not worthwhile speaking. I had said 'Hi!'

"He hadn't answered. I found that I thought 'Poor guy— what a horrid state to be in. I shall do something about this ridiculous state of affairs.'

"So, in my imagination, I stopped right there and re-did

the scene. I said 'Hi!' He answered 'Hi!' and smiled. I now thought 'Good old Ed.'

"I ran the scene over a couple of times and went on to the next incident and finished up the day.

"'Now what—do we do my foot or the concert?'

"I had been melting and wrapping up a wonderful present of courage and success for a friend who was to make her debut the following day and I had been looking forward to giving it to her tonight. My imagination sounded a little bit solemn as it said 'Let us do the concert. It will be more fun.'

"But first couldn't we just take my perfectly good imagination foot out of this physical one before we start?' I pleaded. 'By all means.'

"That done, I had a lovely time at the concert and my friend got a tremendous ovation.

"By now I was very, very sleepy and fell asleep doing my project. The next morning, as I was putting on my slipper, I suddenly had a quick memory picture of withdrawing a discolored and swollen foot from the same slipper. I took my foot out and looked at it. It was perfectly normal in every respect. There was a tiny pink spot on the instep where I remembered I had hit it with the chair.

"'What a vivid dream that was!' I thought and dressed. While waiting for my coffee, I wandered over to my drafting table and saw that all my brushes were lying helter-skelter and unwashed. 'Whatever possessed you to leave your brushes like that?'

"'Don't you remember? It was because of your foot.'

"So it hadn't been a dream after all, but a beautiful healing."

She had won by the art of revision what she would never have won by force.

*In Heaven, the only Art of Living Is Forgetting &
Forgiving. Especially to the Female. [Blake]*

We should take our life, not as it appears to be, but from the vision of this artist, from the vision of the world made perfect that is buried under all minds—buried and waiting for us to revise the day.

We are led to believe a lie when we see with, not through the eye. [Blake]

A revision of the day, and what she held to be so stubbornly real was no longer so to her and, like a dream, had quietly faded away.

You can revise the day to please yourself and by experiencing in imagination the revised speech and actions not only modify the trend of your life story but turn all its discords into harmonies.

The one who discovers the secret of revision cannot do otherwise than let himself be guided by love.

Your effectiveness will increase with practice. Revision is the way by which right can find its appropriate might.

"Resist not evil" [Matt. 5:39], for all passionate conflicts result in an interchange of characteristics.

To him that knoweth to do good, and doeth it not, to him it is sin. [James 4:17]

To know the truth, you must live the truth, and to live the truth, your inner actions must match the actions of your fulfilled desire.

Expectancy and desire must become one.

Your outer world is only actualized inner movement.

Through ignorance of the law of revision, those who take to warfare are perpetually defeated.

Only concepts that idealize depict the truth.

Your ideal of man is his truest self. It is because I firmly believe that whatever is most profoundly imaginative is, in reality, most directly practical that I ask you to live imaginatively and to think into, and to personally appropriate the transcendent saying

"Christ in you, the hope of glory." [Col. 1:27]

Don't blame; only resolve.

It is not man and the earth at their loveliest, but you practicing the art of revision make paradise.

The evidence of this truth can lie only in your own experience of it.

Try revising the day. It is to the pruning shears of revision that we owe our prime fruit.

] 5 [

THE COIN OF HEAVEN

"Does a firm persuasion that a thing is so, make it so?" And the prophet replied, "All poets believe that it does. And in ages of imagination, this firm persuasion removed mountains: but many are not capable of a firm persuasion of anything."

—BLAKE. *MARRIAGE OF HEAVEN AND HELL*

Let every man be fully persuaded in his own mind.

—ROMANS 14:5

Persuasion is an inner effort of intense attention.

To listen attentively as though you heard is to evoke, to activate.

By listening, you can hear what you want to hear and persuade those beyond the range of the outer ear. Speak it inwardly in your imagination only.

Make your inner conversation match your fulfilled desire. What you desire to hear without, you must hear within.

Embrace the without within and become one who hears only that which implies the fulfillment of his desire, and all the external happenings in the world will become a bridge leading to the objective realization of your desire.

Your inner speech is perpetually written all around you in happenings.

Learn to relate these happenings to your inner speech and you will become self-taught.

By inner speech is meant those mental conversations which you carry on with yourself.

They may be inaudible when you are awake because of the noise and distractions of the outer world of becoming, but they are quite audible in deep meditation and dream.

But whether they be audible or inaudible, you are their author and fashion your world in their likeness.

There is a God in heaven [and heaven is within you] that revealeth secrets, and maketh known to the king Nebuchadnezzar what shall be in the latter days. Thy dream, and the visions of thy head upon thy bed, are these. [Dan. 2:28]

Inner speech from premises of fulfilled desire is the way to create an intelligible world for yourself.

Observe your inner speech for it is the cause of future action. Inner speech reveals the state of consciousness from which you view the world.

Make your inner speech match your fulfilled desire, for your inner speech is manifested all around you in happenings.

If any man offend not in word, the same is a perfect man and able also to bridle the whole body. Behold, we put bits in the horses' mouths, that they may obey us: and we turn about their whole body. Behold also the ships, which though they be so great, and are driven by fierce winds, yet are they turned about with a very small helm, whithersoever the governor listeth. Even so the tongue is a little member, and boasteth great things. Behold, how great a matter a little fire kindleth! [James 3:2–5]

The whole manifested world goes to show us what use we have made of the Word—Inner Speech.

An uncritical observation of our inner talking will reveal to us the ideas from which we view the world.

Inner talking mirrors our imagination, and our imagination mirrors the state with which it is fused. If the state with which we are fused is the cause of the phenomenon of our life, then we are relieved of the burden of wondering what to do, for we have no alternative but to identify ourselves with our aim, and inasmuch as the state with which we are identified mirrors itself in our inner speech, then to change the state with which we are fused, we must first change our inner talking.

It is our inner conversations which make tomorrow's facts.

Put off the former conversation, the old man, which is corrupt . . . and be renewed in the spirit of your mind . . . put on the new man, which is created in righteousness. [Eph. 4:22–24]

Our minds, like our stomachs, are whetted by change of food. [Quintillian]

Stop all of the old mechanical negative inner talking and start a new positive and constructive inner speech from premises of fulfilled desire. Inner talking is the beginning, the sowing of the seeds of future action. To determine the action, you must consciously initiate and control your inner talking.

Construct a sentence which implies the fulfillment of your aim, such as "I have a large, steady, dependable income, consistent with integrity and mutual benefit", or "I am happily married", "I am wanted", "I am contributing to the good of the world", and repeat such a sentence over and over until you are inwardly affected by it. Our inner speech represents in various ways the world we live in.

In the beginning was the Word. [John 1:1]

That which ye sow ye reap. See yonder fields! The sesamum was sesamum, the corn was corn. The Silence and the Darkness knew! So is a man's fate born. [*The Light of Asia*, Edwin Arnold]

Ends run true to origins.

Those that go searching for love only make manifest their own lovelessness. And the loveless never find love, only the loving find love, and they never have to seek for it. [D. H. Lawrence]

Man attracts what he *is*. The art of life is to sustain the feeling of the wish fulfilled and let things come to you, not to go after them or think they flee away.

Observe your inner talking and remember your aim. Do they match?

Does your inner talking match what you would say audibly had you achieved your goal?

The individual's inner speech and actions attract the conditions of his life.

Through uncritical self-observation of your inner talking you find where you are in the inner world, and where you are in the inner world is what you are in the outer world.

You put on the new man whenever ideals and inner speech match. In this way alone can the new man be born.

Inner talking matures in the dark.

From the dark it issues into the light. The right inner

speech is the speech that would be yours were you to realize your ideal. In other words, it is the speech of fulfilled desire.

"*I am that.*" [Exod. 3:14]

> There are two gifts which God has bestowed upon man alone, and on no other mortal creature. These two are mind and speech; and the gift of mind and speech is equivalent to that of immortality. If a man uses these two gifts rightly, he will differ in nothing from the immortals . . . and when he quits the body, mind and speech will be his guides, and by them he will be brought into the troop of the gods and the souls that have attained to bliss. [*Hermetica*, Walter Scott's translation]

The circumstances and conditions of life are outpictured inner talking, solidified sound. Inner speech calls events into existence. In every event is the creative sound that is its life and being.

All that a man believes and consents to as true reveals itself in his inner speech. It is his Word, his life.

Try to notice what you are saying in yourself at this moment, to what thoughts and feelings you are consenting. They will be perfectly woven into your tapestry of life. To change your life, you must change your inner talking, for "life", said Hermes, "is the union of Word and Mind".

When imagination matches your inner speech to fulfilled desire, there will then be a straight path in yourself from within out, and the without will instantly reflect the within for you, and you will know reality is only actualized inner talking.

Receive with meekness the inborn Word which is able to save your souls. [James 1:21]

Every stage of man's progress is made by the conscious exercise of his imagination matching his inner speech to his fulfilled desire.

Because man does not perfectly match them, the results are uncertain, while they might be perfectly certain. Persistent assumption of the wish fulfilled is the means of fulfilling the intention.

As we control our inner talking, matching it to our fulfilled desires, we can lay aside all other processes. Then we simply act by clear imagination and intention.

We imagine the wish fulfilled and carry on mental conversations from that premise.

Through controlled inner talking from premises of fulfilled desire, seeming miracles are performed.

The future becomes the present and reveals itself in our inner speech.

To be held by the inner speech of fulfilled desire is to be safely anchored in life.

Our lives may seem to be broken by events, but they are never broken so long as we retain the inner speech of fulfilled desire.

All happiness depends on the active voluntary use of imagination to construct and inwardly affirm that we are what we want to be. We match ourselves to our ideals by constantly remembering our aim and identifying ourselves with it. We fuse with our aims by frequently occupying the feeling of our wish fulfilled.

It is the frequency, the habitual occupancy, that is the secret of success. The oftener we do it, the more natural it is. Fancy assembles. Continuous imagination fuses.

It is possible to resolve every situation by the proper use of imagination.

Our task is to get the right sentence, the one which implies that our desire is realized, and fire the imagination with it.

All this is intimately connected with the mystery of "the still small voice".

Inner talking reveals the activities of imagination, activities which are the causes of the circumstances of life.

As a rule, man is totally unaware of his inner talking and therefore sees himself not as the cause but the victim of circumstance.

To consciously create circumstance, man must consciously direct his inner speech, matching "the still small voice" to his fulfilled desires.

He calls things not seen as though they were. [Romans 4:17]

Right inner speech is essential. It is the greatest of the arts. It is the way out of limitation into freedom.

Ignorance of this art has made the world a battlefield and penitentiary where blood and sweat alone are expected, when it should be a place of marveling and wondering.

Right inner talking is the first step to becoming what you want to be.

Speech is an image of mind, and mind is an image of God. [*Hermetica*, Scott translation]

On the morning of April 12, 1953, my wife was awakened by the sound of a great voice of authority speaking within her and saying. "You must stop spending your thoughts, time, and money. Everything in life must be an investment."

To spend is to waste, to squander, to layout without return. To invest is to layout for a purpose from which a profit is expected. This revelation of my wife is about the importance of the moment. It is about the transformation of the moment. What we desire does not lie in the future but in ourselves at this very moment.

At any moment in our lives, we are faced with an infinite choice: "what we are and what we want to be".

And what we want to be is already existent, but to realize it we must match our inner speech and actions to it.

If two of you shall agree on earth as touching anything that they shall ask, it shall be done for them of My Father which is in heaven. [Matt. 18:19]

It is only what is done *now* that counts.

The present moment does not recede into the past. It advances into the future to confront us, spent or invested.

Thought is the coin of heaven. Money is its earthly symbol.

Every moment must be invested, and our inner talking reveals whether we are spending or investing.

Be more interested in what you are inwardly "saying now" than what you "have said" by choosing wisely what you think and what you feel *now.*

Any time we feel misunderstood, misused, neglected, suspicious, afraid, we are spending our thoughts and wasting our time.

Whenever we assume the feeling of being what we want to be, we are investing.

We cannot abandon the moment to negative inner talking and expect to retain command of life.

Before us go the results of all that seemingly is behind. Not gone is the last moment—but oncoming.

My word shall not return unto Me void, but it shall accomplish that which I please, and it shall prosper in the thing whereto I sent it. [Isa. 55:11]

The circumstances of life are the muffled utterances of the inner talking that made them—the word made visible.

"The Word", said Hermes, "is Son, and the Mind is Father of the Word. They are not separate one from the other; for life is the union of Word and Mind."

He willed us forth from Himself by the Word of Truth. [James 1:18]

Let us *be imitators of God as dear children* [Ephesians 5:1], and use our inner speech wisely to mould an outer world in harmony with our ideal.

The Lord spake by me, and His Word was in my tongue. [2 Sam. 23:2]

The mouth of God is the mind of man. Feed God only the best.

Whatsoever things are of good report . . . think on these things. [Phil. 4:8]

The present moment is always precisely right for an investment, to inwardly speak the right word.

The word is very near to you, in your mouth, and in your heart, that you may do it. See, I have set before you this day life and good, death and evil, blessings and cursings. Choose life. [Deut. 30:14, 15, 19]

You choose life and good and blessings by *being* that which you choose. Like is known to like alone.

Make your inner speech bless and give good reports.

Man's ignorance of the future is the result of his ignorance of his inner talking. His inner talking mirrors his imagination, and his imagination is a government in which the opposition never comes into power.

If the reader ask, "What if the inner speech remains subjective and is unable to find an object for its love?", the answer is: it will not remain subjective, for the very simple reason that inner speech is always objectifying itself.

What frustrates and festers and becomes the disease that afflicts humanity is man's ignorance of the art of matching inner words to fulfilled desire.

Inner speech mirrors imagination, and imagination is Christ.

Alter your inner speech, and your perceptual world changes. Whenever inner speech and desire are in conflict, inner speech invariably wins.

Because inner speech objectifies itself, it is easy to see that if it matches desire, desire will be objectively realized. Were this not so, I would say with Blake, Sooner murder an infant in its cradle than nurse unacted desires.

But I know from experience,

The tongue . . . setteth on fire the course of nature. [James 3:6]

] 6 [

IT IS WITHIN

Rivers, Mountains, Cities, Villages,
All are Human, & when you enter into
their Bosoms you walk
In Heavens & Earths, as in your own
Bosom you bear your Heaven
And Earth & all you behold; tho' it
appears Without, it is Within.
In your Imagination, of which this World
of Mortality is but a Shadow.

—BLAKE, *JERUSALEM*

The inner world was as real to Blake as the outer land of
waking life. He looked upon his dreams and visions as
the realities of the forms of nature. Blake reduced everything
to the bedrock of his own consciousness.

The Kingdom of Heaven is within you. [Luke 17:21]

The Real Man, the Imaginative Man, has invested the
outer world with all of its properties. The apparent reality of

the outer world which is so hard to dissolve is only proof of the absolute reality of the inner world of his own imagination.

> *No man can come to me, except the Father which hath*
> *sent Me draw him . . . I and My Father are One.*
> [John 6:44, 10:30]

The world which is described from observation is a manifestation of the mental activity of the observer.

When man discovers that his world is his own mental activity made visible, that no man can come unto him except he draws him, and that there is no one to change but himself, his own imaginative self, his first impulse is to reshape the world in the image of his ideal.

But his ideal is not so easily incarnated. In that moment when he ceases to conform to external discipline, he must impose upon himself a far more rigorous discipline, the self-discipline upon which the realization of his ideal depends.

Imagination is not entirely untrammeled and free to move at will without any rules to constrain it. In fact, the contrary is true. Imagination travels according to habit.

Imagination has choice, but it chooses according to habit. Awake or asleep, man's imagination is constrained to follow certain definite patterns. It is this benumbing influence of habit that man must change; if he does not, his dreams will fade under the paralysis of custom.

Imagination, which is Christ in man, is not subject to the necessity to produce only that which is perfect and good. It exercises its absolute freedom from necessity by endowing the outer physical self with free will to choose to follow good or evil, order or disorder.

Choose this day whom ye will serve. [Joshua 24:15]

But after the choice is made and accepted so that it forms the individual's habitual consciousness, then imagination manifests its infinite power and wisdom by moulding the outer sensuous world of becoming in the image of the habitual inner speech and actions of the individual.

To realize his ideal, man must first change the pattern which his imagination has followed.

Habitual thought is indicative of character.

The way to change the outer world is to make the inner speech and action match the outer speech and action of ful-filled desire.

Our ideals are waiting to be incarnated, but unless we ourselves match our inner speech and action to the speech and action of fulfilled desire, they are incapable of birth.

Inner speech and action are the channels of God's action. He cannot respond to our prayer unless these paths are offered.

The outer behaviour of man is mechanical. It is subject to the compulsion applied to it by the behaviour of the inner self, and old habits of the inner self hang on till replaced by new ones. It is a peculiar property of the second or inner man that he gives to the outer self something similar to his own reality of being. Any change in the behavior of the inner self will result in corresponding outer changes.

The mystic calls a change of consciousness "death". By death he means, not the destruction of imagination and the state with which it was fused, but the dissolution of their union.

Fusion is union rather than oneness. Thus the conditions to

which that union gave being vanish. "I die daily", said Paul to the Corinthians [1 Cor. 15:31]. Blake said to his friend Crabbe Robinson:

> *There is nothing like death. Death is the best thing that can happen in life; but most people die so late and take such an unmerciful time in dying. God knows, their neighbors never see them rise from the dead.*

To the outer man of sense, who knows nothing of the inner man of Being, this is sheer nonsense. But Blake made the above quite clear when he wrote in the year before he died:

William Blake—one who is very much delighted with being in good company.

Born 28 November 1757 in London and has died several times since.

When man has the sense of Christ *as his imagination*, he sees why Christ must die and rise again from the dead to save man—why he must detach his imagination from his present state and match it to a higher concept of himself if he would rise above his present limitations and thereby save himself.

Here is a lovely story of a mystical death which was witnessed by a "neighbor".

"Last week", writes the one "who rose from the dead", "a friend offered me her home in the mountains for the Christmas holidays as she thought she might go east. She said that she would let me know this week. We had a very pleasant conversation and I mentioned you and your teaching in connection with a discussion of Dunne's 'Experiment with Time' which she had been reading.

"Her letter arrived Monday. As I picked it up, I had a sudden sense of depression. However, when I read it, she said I could have the house and told me where to get the keys.

"Instead of being cheerful, I grew still more depressed, so much so I decided there must have been something between the lines which I was getting intuitively. I unfolded the letter and read the first page through and as I turned to the second page, I noticed she had written a postscript on the back of the first sheet. It consisted of an extremely blunt and heavy-handed description of an unlovely trait in my character which I had struggled for years to overcome, and for the past two years I thought I had succeeded.

"Yet here it was again, described with clinical exactitude.

"I was stunned and desolated. I thought to myself, 'What is this letter trying to tell me? In the first place, she invited me to use her house, as I have been seeing myself in some lovely home during the holidays. In the second place, nothing comes to me except I draw it. And thirdly I have been hearing *nothing* but good news. So the obvious conclusion is that something in me corresponds to this letter and no matter what it looks like it is good news.' I reread the letter and as I did so, I asked, 'What is there here for me to see?'

"And then I saw. It started out. 'After our conversation of last week, I feel I can tell you . . .' and the rest of the page was as studded with 'weres' and 'wases' as currants in a seed cake. A great feeling of elation swept over me.

"It was *all* in the past. The thing I had labored so long to correct was *done*. I suddenly realized that my friend was a witness to my resurrection. I whirled around the studio, chanting, 'It's all in the past! It is done. Thank you, it is done!'

"I gathered all my gratitude up in a big ball of light and shot it straight to you and if you saw a flash of lightning Monday evening shortly after six your time, that was it.

"Now, instead of writing a polite letter because it is the correct thing to do. I can write giving sincere thanks for her frankness and thanking her for the loan of her house.

"Thank you so much for your teaching, which has made my beloved imagination truly my Saviour."

And now, if any man shall say unto her "Lo, here is Christ, or there" [Matt. 24:23], she will believe it not, for she knows that the Kingdom of God is within her and that she herself must assume full responsibility for the incarnation of her ideal and that nothing but death and resurrection will bring her to it.

She has found her Saviour, her beloved Imagination, forever expanding in the bosom of God.

There is only one reality, and that is Christ—Human Imagination, the inheritance and final achievement of the whole of Humanity,

That we . . . speaking the truth in love, may grow up into Him in all things, which is the head, even Christ. [Eph. 4:14, 15]

CREATION IS FINISHED

I am the beginning and the end, there is nothing to come that
has not been, and is.

—ECCLESIASTES 3:15 ERV

B LAKE SAW all possible human situations as "already-
made" *states*. He saw every aspect, every plot and drama
as already worked out as "mere possibilities" as long as we are
not in them, but as overpowering realities when we are in
them.

He described these states as "Sculptures of Los's Halls".

*Distinguish therefore states from Individuals in those States.
States change but Individual Identities never change nor cease . . .
The Imagination is not a State.*

Said Blake,

*It is the Human Existence itself. Affection or Love becomes a
State when divided from imagination.*

Just how important this is to remember is almost impossible to say, but the moment the individual realizes this for

the first time is the most momentous in his life, and to be encouraged to feel this is the highest form of encouragement it is possible to give.

This truth is common to all men, but the consciousness of it—and much more, the self-consciousness of it—is another matter.

The day I realized this great truth—that everything in my world is a manifestation of the mental activity which goes on within me, and that the conditions and circumstances of my life only reflect the state of consciousness with which I am fused—is the most momentous in my life.

But the experience that brought me to this certainty is so remote from ordinary existence, I have long hesitated to tell it, for my reason refused to admit the conclusions to which the experience impelled me. Nevertheless, this experience revealed to me that I am supreme within the circle of my own state of consciousness and that it is the state with which I am identified that determines what I experience.

Therefore it should be shared with all, for to know this is to become free from the world's greatest tyranny, the belief in a second cause.

Blessed are the pure in heart: for they shall see God. [Matt. 5:8]

Blessed are they whose imagination has been so purged of the beliefs in second causes they know that imagination is all, and all is imagination.

One day I quietly slipped from my apartment in New York City into some remote yesteryear's countryside. As I entered the dining room of a large inn, I became fully conscious. I knew that my physical body was immobilized on my bed back in New York.

Yet here I was as awake and as conscious as I have ever been. I intuitively knew that if I could stop the activity of my mind, everything before me would freeze. No sooner was the thought born than the urge to try it possessed me. I felt my head tighten, then thicken to a stillness. My attention concentrated into a crystal-clear focus, and the waitress walking, walked not. And I looked through the window and the leaves falling, fell not. And the family of four eating, ate not. And they lifting the food, lifted it not. Then my attention relaxed, the tightness eased, and of a sudden all moved onward in their course. The leaves fell, the waitress walked and the family ate. Then I understood Blake's vision of the "Sculptures of Los's Halls".

I sent you to reap that whereon ye bestowed no labor. [John 4:38] Creation is finished.

I am the beginning and the end, there is nothing to come that has not been, and is. [Eccles. 3:15, ERV]

The world of creation is finished and its original is within us.

We saw it before we set forth, and have since been trying to remember it and to activate sections of it. There are infinite views of it. Our task is to get the right view and by determined direction of our attention make it pass in procession before the inner eye. If we assemble the right sequence and experience it in imagination until it has the tone of reality, then we consciously create circumstances.

This inner procession is the activity of imagination that must be consciously directed. We, by a series of mental transformations, become aware of increasing portions of that which already is, and by matching our own mental activity to that portion of creation which we desire to experience, we activate it, resurrect it, and give it life.

This experience of mine not only shows the world as a manifestation of the mental activity of the individual observer, but it also reveals our course of time as jumps of attention between eternal moments. An infinite abyss separates any two moments of ours.

We, by the movements of our attention, give life to the "Sculptures of Los's Halls".

Think of the world as containing an infinite number of states of consciousness from which it could be viewed. Think of these states as rooms or mansions in the House of God [John 14:2], and like the rooms of any house, they are fixed relative to one another.

But think of yourself, the Real Self, the Imaginative You, as the living, moving occupant of God's House.

Each room contains some of Los's Sculptures, with infinite plots and dramas and situations already worked out but not activated.

They are activated as soon as Human Imagination enters and fuses with them. Each represents certain mental and emotional activities. To enter a state, man must consent to the ideas and feelings which it represents.

These states represent an infinite number of possible mental transformations which man can experience. To move into another state or mansion necessitates a change of beliefs.

All that you could ever desire is already present and only waits to be matched by your beliefs.

But it must be matched, for that is the necessary condition by which alone it can be activated and objectified.

Matching the beliefs of a state is the seeking that finds, the knocking to which it is opened, the asking that receives [Matt. 7:8; Luke 11:10]. *Go in and possess the land* [Exod. 6:4–8].

The moment man matches the beliefs of any state, he fuses with it, and this union results in the activation and projection of its plots, plans, dramas, and situations.

It becomes the individual's home from which he views the world. It is his workshop, and, if he is observant, he will see outer reality shaping itself upon the model of his . . . Imagination.

It is for this purpose of training us in image-making that we were made subject to the limitations of the senses and clothed in bodies of flesh.

It is the awakening of the imagination, the returning of His Son, that our Father waits for.

The creature was made subject to vanity not willingly, but by reason of him who subjected it. [Rom. 8:20]

But the victory of the Son, the return of the prodigal, assures us that

the creature shall be delivered from the bondage of corruption into the glorious liberty of the Sons [children] of God. [Rom. 8:21]

We were subjected to this biological experience because no one can know of imagination who has not been subjected to the vanities and limitations of the flesh, who has not taken his share of Sonship and gone prodigal, who has not experimented and tasted this cup of experience; and confusion will continue until man awakes and a fundamentally imaginative view of life has been reestablished and acknowledged as basic.

I should preach . . . the unsearchable riches of Christ and make all men see what is the fellowship of the mystery, which from the beginning of the world has been hid in God, Who created all things by Jesus Christ. [Eph. 3:8, 9]

Bear in mind that Christ in you is your imagination.

As the appearance of our world is determined by the particular state with which we are fused, so may we determine our fate as individuals by fusing our imaginations with ideals we seek to realize. On the distinction between our states of consciousness depends the distinction between the circumstances and conditions of our lives.

Man, who is free in his choice of state, often cries out to be saved from the state of his choice.

And ye shall cry out in that day, because of your king which ye shall have chosen you; and the Lord will not hear you in that day. Nevertheless, the people refused to obey the voice of Samuel; and they said, Nay; but we will have a king over us. [1 Sam. 8:18, 19]

Choose wisely the state that you will serve. All states are lifeless until imagination fuses with them.

All things when they are admitted are made manifest by the light: for everything that is made manifest is light [Eph. 5:13],

and

Ye are the light of the world [Matt. 5:14],

by which those ideas to which you have consented are made manifest.

Hold fast to your ideal. Nothing can take it from you but your imagination.

Don't think *of* your ideal, think *from* it. It is only the ideals *from* which you think that are ever realized.

Man lives not by bread alone, but by every word that proceeds out of the mouth of God [Matt. 4:4], and "the mouth of God" is the mind of man.

Become a drinker and an eater of the ideals you wish to

realize. Have a set, definite aim or your mind will wander, and wandering it eats every negative suggestion.

If you live right mentally, everything else will be right.

By a change of mental diet, you can alter the course of observed events.

But unless there is a change of mental diet, your personal history remains the same. You illuminate or darken your life by the ideas to which you consent.

Nothing is more important to you than the ideas on which you feed. And you feed on the ideas *from* which you think. If you find the world unchanged, it is a sure sign that you are wanting in fidelity to the new mental diet, which you neglect in order to condemn your environment. You are in need of a new and sustained attitude.

You can be anything you please if you will make the conception habitual, for any idea which excludes all others from the field of attention discharges in action.

The ideas and moods to which you constantly return define the state with which you are fused.

Therefore train yourself to occupy more frequently the feeling of your wish fulfilled.

This is creative magic. It is the way to work toward fusion with the desired state.

If you would assume the feeling of your wish fulfilled more frequently, you would be master of your fate, *but unfortunately you shut out your assumption for all but the occasional hour.* Practice making real to yourself the feeling of the wish fulfilled.

After you have assumed the feeling of the wish fulfilled, do not close the experience as you would a book, but carry it around like a fragrant odor.

Instead of being completely forgotten, let it remain in the

atmosphere communicating its influence automatically to your actions and reactions. A mood, often repeated, gains a momentum that is hard to break or check. So be careful of the feelings you entertain. Habitual moods reveal the state with which you are fused.

It is always possible to pass from thinking *of* the end you desire to realize, to thinking *from* the end.

But the crucial matter is thinking *from* the end, for thinking *from* means unification or fusion with the idea: whereas in thinking *of* the end, there is always subject and object—the thinking individual and the thing thought. You must imagine yourself into the state of your wish fulfilled, in your love for that state, and in so doing, live and think *from* it and no more *of* it. You pass from thinking *of* to thinking *from* by centering your imagination in the feeling of the wish fulfilled.

] 8 [

THE APPLE OF GOD'S EYE

What think ye of the Christ? Whose Son is He?

—MATTHEW 22:42

When this question is asked of you, let your answer be, "Christ is my imagination", and, though I

See not yet all things put under him [Heb. 2:8],

yet I know that I am Mary from whom sooner or later He shall be born, and eventually

Do all things through Christ [Phil. 4:13].

The birth of Christ is the awakening of the inner or Second man. It is becoming conscious of the mental activity within oneself, which activity continues whether we are conscious of it or not.

The birth of Christ does not bring any person from a distance, or make anything to be that was not there before. It is the unveiling of the Son of God in man. The Lord "cometh in clouds" [Mark 13:26; Luke 21:27] is the prophet's description of the pulsating rings of golden liquid light on the head of him in whom He awakes. The coming is from within and not from without, as Christ is *in* us [Rom. 8:10; 2 Cor. 13:3; Gal. 2:20, 4:19; Col. 1:27].

This great mystery

God was manifest in the flesh [1 Tim. 3:16]

begins with Advent, and it is appropriate that the cleansing of the Temple,

Which temple ye are, [1 Cor. 3:17],

stands in the forefront of the Christian mysteries:

The Kingdom of Heaven is within you. [Luke 17:21]

Advent is unveiling the mystery of your being. If you will practice the art of revision by a life lived according to the wise, imaginative use of your inner speech and inner actions, in confidence that by the conscious use of *"the power that worketh in us"* [Eph. 3:20], Christ will awake in you; if you believe it, trust it, act upon it; Christ will awake in you. This is Advent.

Great is the mystery, God was manifest in the flesh. [1 Tim. 3:16]

From Advent on, *He that toucheth you toucheth the apple of God's eye.* [Zech. 2:8]

ABOUT THE AUTHOR

Neville Goddard (1905–1972) abandoned his work as a dancer and actor to dedicate himself to a career as a metaphysical writer and lecturer. Neville's work, including his book *At Your Command*, influenced a range of spiritual thinkers from Joseph Murphy to Carlos Castaneda.